# *The Bible:*

## Its Necessity, Qualities & Use

# The Bible:

## Its Necessity, Qualities & Use

by

**Roy Mohon**

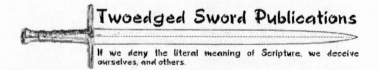

Twoedged Sword Publications

If we deny the literal meaning of Scripture, we deceive ourselves, and others.

First published 2006

ISBN-13   978-1-905447-09-1

ISBN-10   1-905447-09-4

Twoedged Sword Publications
PO Box 266, Waterlooville, PO7 5ZT
www.twoedgedswordpublications.co.uk

## ACKNOWLEDGEMENTS

Quotations from John Owen, *Biblical Theology: The History of Theology From Adam to Christ or The Nature, Origin, Development, and Study of Theological Truth, In Six Books* translated by Stephen P. Westcott (Morgan, PA: Soli Deo Gloria Publications, 1994) by kind permission of the publisher.

Quotations from the *Word List* published in the *Quarterly Record* Number 571 (April to June 2005) and Psalm 19 from the Metrical Psalter by kind permission of the *Trinitarian Bible Society*.

Cover Design by Abby2.com "Is not my word... like a hammer that breaketh the rock in pieces?"

# CONTENTS

# Chapter 1

## *The Necessity Of Scripture: There Is No Other Saving Revelation*

*The Light of Nature – Revelation in the Works of Creation and Providence – All Inexcusable – General Revelation is not Sufficient to Give Saving Knowledge*

The man or woman suffering from a physical disease that will prove terminal, unless treated by the *one* available remedy, will not be interested in false claims to provide a cure. He or she knows that the effective remedy is essential and that it will be futile to seek an alternative where none exists. It is sad that sinners do not apply the same logic to the matter of salvation but often pin their hopes of eternal life upon some natural religion instead of upon the teachings of Scripture. It is, however, made crystal clear in the Christian Gospel that it is only in Scripture that the remedy for sin is found and that all efforts to derive saving knowledge from the exploration of the universe are in vain.

In its first chapter the *Westminster Confession of Faith* states:

> 'Although the light of nature and the works of creation and providence do so far manifest the goodness, wisdom, and power of God, as to leave men unexcusable; yet are they not sufficient to give that knowledge of God and of His will, which is necessary unto salvation. Therefore it pleased the Lord, at sundry times, and in divers manners, to reveal Himself, and to declare that His will unto His Church; and afterwards, for the better preserving and propagating of the truth, and for the more sure establishment and comfort of the Church against the corruption of the flesh, and the malice of Satan and of the world, to commit the same wholly unto writing; which maketh the Holy Scripture to be

most necessary; those former ways of God's revealing His
will unto His people being now ceased.'[1]

This opening paragraph of the Confession follows the Bible in avoiding
any debate concerning the existence of God. There is no attempt to
present any philosophical arguments to prove that a Divine Being exists.
As Professor Louis Berkhof explains: 'For us the existence of God is the
great presupposition of theology. There is no sense in speaking of the
knowledge of God, unless it may be assumed that God exists. The
presupposition of Christian theology is of a very definite type. The
assumption is not merely that there is something, some idea or ideal, some
power or purposeful tendency, to which the name of God may be applied,
but that there is a self-existent, self-conscious, personal Being, which is
the origin of all things, and which transcends the entire creation, but is at
the same time immanent in every part of it.'[2] Scripture warrants this
presupposition. Moses proceeds similarly in the first book of the Bible.
In Genesis chapters 1 and 2 no effort is made to prove by argumentation
that God exists. The whole of the creation record presupposes that *he is*.[3]
Moses sets out, not to prove God's existence, but to record his works. As
we shall see, those works provide such evidence of the Being of God that
not to believe in him is inexcusable.

The starting point of the Confession should be compared with the first
two chapters of Paul's *Epistle to the Romans* because the proof texts[4]
show that the framers of the Confession had this epistle in mind. This
letter was intended by the Apostle Paul to provide a systematic
exposition of the Gospel he preached. The theme of Paul's letter to the
Romans, as announced after his greetings, is fully evangelical. He is
concerned with 'the gospel of Christ' which 'is the power of God unto
salvation to everyone that believeth; to the Jew first, and also to the
Greek.'[5] Paul is setting out an orderly doctrinal statement of the message

---

[1] The Confession of Faith of the Westminster Assembly of Divines' Chapter 1.1 in
S. W. Carruthers (ed.), *The Westminster Confession of Faith* (Manchester: R. Aikman
& Son, 1937) p. 89.

[2] L. Berkhof, *Systematic Theology* (Edinburgh: The Banner of Truth Trust, 1963) pp. 20–21.

[3] Hebrews 11.6.

[4] Romans 2.14–15, 1.19–20.

[5] Romans 1.16.

of salvation. In this exposition he commences, not with Christ and redemption, but with man's condition as a creature of God faced with a clear revelation of his Maker. This is not incompatible with Paul's missionary task. There is something vitally important about the whole matter of revelation. Whatever knowledge of God sinners might have in their fallen state, that knowledge can only condemn them, it cannot save them. The Confession follows Paul in this starting point. At the very outset there is an urgent question as to where an authoritative saving revelation of God can be found. It is this that leads on to the necessity of redemptive revelation and the preservation of the truth in written form but, following the example of Paul, the Westminster Divines first dealt with the subject of the revelation of God the Creator.

If we analyze the content of the opening paragraph of the Confession we see the following:

> *The need for the Bible arises because the revelation of God
> the Creator cannot save sinners.*

God is made known to us in various ways: (a) by the light of nature and (b) by his works of creation and providence. By these different ways Divine perfections are revealed to us such as: (a) the goodness of God, (b) the wisdom of God, and (c) the power of God. We consequently have no excuse for not worshipping our Creator but this revelation does not make God known to us as Saviour and the revelation of God the Creator cannot save sinners.

> *The need for the Bible arises because the preservation and
> proclamation of saving truth in the face of the attacks of the
> world, the flesh and the Devil is better served by a written
> revelation.*

God has revealed Himself as Saviour in a variety of ways to his Church. But his purpose of salvation is better served by written revelation because (a) it provides for the preservation of saving truth, and (b) it provides for the proclamation of saving truth. It thus provides for the comfort of the Church against: (a) the flesh, (b) the malice of Satan, and (c) the malice of the world.

> *The need for the Bible arises because the fragmentary
> revelations of the way of salvation have ceased.*

11

## THE LIGHT OF NATURE

### Romans 2.14–15

'For when the Gentiles, which have not the law, do by nature the things contained in the law, these, having not the law, are a law unto themselves: Which shew the work of the law written in their hearts, their conscience also bearing witness, and their thoughts the mean while accusing or else excusing one another...'

In this passage the Apostle Paul is dealing with the *Gentiles*. This term covers everyone who is not a Jew. The Gentiles did not have the Law as given by Moses but Paul intends to show that this did not mean that they were without the Law of God in every sense. Even though they did not have the Pentateuch and the Ten Commandments Paul states that they showed *the work of the law written in their hearts*. There is a great moral challenge in these words. As Calvin explains: 'That there exists in the human mind, and indeed by natural instinct, some sense of Deity, we hold to be beyond dispute, since God himself, to prevent any man from pretending ignorance, has endued all men with some idea of his Godhead, the memory of which he constantly renews and occasionally enlarges, that all to a man, being aware that there is a God, and that he is their Maker, may be condemned by their own conscience when they neither worship him nor consecrate their lives to his service.'[6] In dealing with the Apostle's words we will consider: (1) the *presence* of law in the absence of the Law, (2) that the *proof* of this is seen in human behaviour and (3) the *personal significance* for each one of us.

### The *Presence* of Law in the Absence of the Law

The common meaning of the phrase *a law unto themselves* is not what is intended by Paul. We use such words of those who go their own way and make up their own rules as they go along. Paul is using it in an opposite sense. He is saying that the moral law of God is so firmly embedded in our nature that, despite the corruption of sin, we cannot escape from it.

---

[6] John Calvin, *Institutes of the Christian Religion*, Volume One (London: James Clarke & Co., Limited, 1962) p. 43.

Although the heathen nations did not have the written law of Moses, they nevertheless were found to do many things contained in it. All the heathen did not murder others, commit adulterous acts or live by theft. The Gentile nations did not have the specifically revealed law that God gave to Israel through Moses, written upon stone tablets or in the books of Moses. However, what is required by that law is *written* in the hearts of everyone, so that our own moral nature includes the voice of conscience, which refers to this law within us to commend what is good and accuse us when we do what is bad or evil.

## The *Proof* of this is Seen in Human Behaviour

The Gentiles *do by nature the things contained in the law.* We have what Professor Murray calls a 'native instinct' or 'spontaneous impulse' to do certain things the law requires.[7] We do not do all that the Law of God requires, neither do we do anything perfectly; but various aspects of human behaviour show *the work of the law* written in our hearts. People try to be good and have certain standards about honesty, faithfulness and so on. They look after their families and help friends who are ill.

## The *Personal Significance* for each one of us

Because we are moral creatures, unlike animals that are not, we are not altogether ignorant of God's law. Our consciences approve what is good and accuse us of our evil deeds by reference to this law. Acquaintance with the Bible is not needed for this to take place. Everyone's conscience tells the same story. Whatever can be approved of in anyone's life, there is so much that is against the perfect requirements of God. All non-Jews are in the same condition: 'as many as have sinned without law shall also perish without law...'[8]

In summarizing we can say that God is our Lawgiver. We all have *some* knowledge of his law. None of us can plead the excuse of ignorance when we break God's law. We show by our behaviour that we know in some respect what his law requires. Our consciences tell us what is good

---

[7] John Murray, *The Epistle to the Romans: The English Text with Introduction, Exposition and Notes* (Grand Rapids: Wm. B. Eerdmans Publishing Co., 1968) p.73.

[8] Romans 2.12.

and accuse us for our own misdeeds. The consequence is obvious: without forgiveness we will all perish and therefore we all need the Gospel.

## REVELATION IN THE WORKS OF CREATION AND PROVIDENCE

### *Romans 1.19–20*

'Because that which may be known of God is manifest in them; for God hath shewed it unto them. For the invisible things of him from the creation of the world are clearly seen, being understood by the things that are made, even his eternal power and Godhead; so that they are without excuse...'

### *Psalm 19.1–3*

'The heavens declare the glory of God; and the firmament[9] sheweth his handywork. Day unto day uttereth speech, and night unto night sheweth knowledge. There is no speech nor language, where their voice is not heard.'

God makes himself known in the world about us in a way that everyone can see. As the author is known by his books and the architect is known by his buildings so *that which may be known of God* is seen in the universe day by day and the very sky above our heads witnesses to God's glory. John Calvin explains: 'Since the perfection of blessedness consists in the knowledge of God, he has been pleased, in order that none might be excluded from the means of obtaining felicity, not only to deposit in our minds that seed of religion of which we have already spoken, but so to manifest his perfections in the whole structure of the universe, and daily place himself in our view, that we cannot open our eyes without being compelled to behold him. His essence, indeed, is incomprehensible, utterly transcending all human thought; but on each of his works his glory is engraven in characters so bright, so distinct, and so illustrious, that none, however dull and illiterate, can plead ignorance as their excuse.'[10] We will

---

[9] The *firmament* is 'the vault of heaven', the vast expanse *spread out* above our heads.

[10] John Calvin, *op. cit.*, p.51.

consider the following: (1) the *characteristics* of this revelation, (2) that the *content* of the revelation is important, and (3) that the *consequence* of this revelation is very serious.

## The *Characteristics* of this Revelation

The universe is used by God to make himself known. *The invisible things of him* are understood *by the things that are made.* The older writers spoke of a revelation in things. This revelation is *uninterrupted.* Ever since the creation (*from* in a temporal sense), through all history, there has been an uninterrupted testimony from one day to the next, telling out continually the glory of God. The revelation is *unrestrained.* Each day *uttereth* speech. The Hebrew involves the idea of 'flowing' like a stream. We can think of the speech bubbling forth with energetic abundance like that of the mountain spring. This revelation is *universal.* It reaches to everyone everywhere, men, women, boys and girls, whether scholars or without learning. All can understand it. Their *voice is heard.* Dumb creatures surmount all language barriers and effectively communicate knowledge of God.

No nation is exempt from this forceful penetration of truth. That *which may be known of God* is *manifest in them*; God has *shewed it* to them. The invisible things of God *are clearly seen,* being *understood.* Nothing could be plainer. Thus Francis Turretin comments: 'Now he is blind who does not see the most beautiful order everywhere and most wicked who does not acknowledge it. There is so suitable a disposition of parts, so constant a concord of things so discordant, so harmonious an agreement and consent of creatures the most diverse, so swift and at the same time equable motion of the heavenly bodies and so immutable a stability and constancy of the order once established. So not only do the heavens declare the glory of God, but every blade of grass and flower in the field, every pebble on the shore and every shell in the ocean proclaim not only his power and goodness, but also his manifold wisdom, so near each one that even by feeling, God can be found.'[11]

---

[11] Francis Turretin, *Institutes of Elenctic Theology,* Volume 1 (Phillipsburg, New Jersey: P&R Publishing, 1992) pp. 171–172.

## The *Content* of the Revelation is Important.

It is the *glory of God* the Creator that is revealed. The effect points us to the only adequate Cause. The birthday cake arose because of a mother's kindness. Even the wildest explanations of the origins of Stonehenge do not suggest that it arose by chance. The evidences of design point to intelligence. When we see the wrought iron we know that the strong arm of the blacksmith has been at work. Why then should anyone want to deny that 'the works of creation and providence' show 'the goodness, wisdom and power of God'? The evidence of creation is clear enough and the truth must be suppressed in order to evade the unmistakable testimony. The universe reveals the Creator's *eternal power and Godhead* showing: (1) His *eternity* as the One beyond space and time. (2) His *almightiness* as he who brings out the stars of heaven as an army calling 'them all by names by the greatness of his might.' As he is 'strong in power; not one faileth.'[12] (3) His *Divinity* as infinitely perfect, immortal, wise and good.

## The *Consequence* of this Revelation is Very Serious.

Paul plainly states the result of unbelief: 'For the invisible things of him from the creation of the world are clearly seen, being understood by the things that are made, even his eternal power and Godhead; *so that they are without excuse...*' For man in his original integrity, such a revelation would result in deep happiness and blessing. As far as fallen human beings are concerned this revelation results in inexcusability. The emotive complaint that it would be unjust for God to condemn uncivilized tribes in remote places because they have had no opportunity to hear the Gospel and believe cannot be allowed to stand. The Apostle Paul says exactly the opposite. Rejection and distortion of the truth about God shows the truth *about us*. We are fallen creatures 'who hold the truth in unrighteousness.'[13] The Gentiles, whether educated or uneducated, showed themselves in their true colours, because, 'when they knew God, they glorified him not as God, neither were thankful; but became vain in their imaginations, and their foolish heart was darkened. Professing

---

[12] Isaiah 40.26.

[13] Romans 1.18.

themselves to be wise, they became fools, And changed the glory of the uncorruptible God into an image made like to corruptible man...'[14] It all has a very contemporary ring, revealing that, in our natural condition:

> We are not objective in our thinking but *biased*.

> We are not ignorant but *disobedient*.

> We are not wise but *foolish*.

> We are not innocent but *inexcusable*.

> We are not in control but *condemned*.

Robert Shaw sums up the significance of the knowledge of God attainable by the light of nature. 'It is a testimony of the goodness of God towards his creatures... As it shows men their duty, and convinces them of sin, in many points; so it has some influence on mankind, at least by the fear of punishment, in restraining them from extreme degrees of wickedness... It excites men to seek after a clearer revelation of God, and prepares the way for their receiving the gospel of his grace... It serves to vindicate the conduct of God as a righteous governor, in his severe dealing with obstinate sinners, both here and hereafter. This will leave them without excuse in the great day, when God shall judge the secrets of all hearts.'[15]

## ALL INEXCUSABLE

### *Romans 1.32, with chap. 2.1*

> 'Who knowing the judgment of God, that they which commit such things are worthy of death, not only do the same, but have pleasure in them that do them. Therefore thou art inexcusable, O man, whosoever thou art that judgest: for wherein thou judgest another, thou condemnest thyself; for thou that judgest doest the same things.'

---

[14] Romans 1.21–23.

[15] Robert Shaw, *The Reformed Faith: An Exposition of the Confession of Faith of the Westminster Assembly of Divines* (Inverness: Christian Focus Publications, 1973) p.4.

There are three challenges in these verses: (1) *Committing* sins makes us inexcusable. (2) *Continuing* in sins makes us more inexcusable. (3) *Condemning* ourselves shows that we are inexcusable.

### *Committing* Sins Makes us Inexcusable

The truth about our situation has to be faced. Through the created universe God is made known to us in his rich goodness as our Benefactor, in his amazing wisdom as the Architect of the cosmos and in his omnipotence as its Governor. Such sovereign glory demands unceasing praise from us, but none of us in our natural condition worship God properly. Although there is a measure of readiness to accept some concept of an ultimate truth beyond the world undergirding everything, which the philosopher might call the Absolute, the truth about the real God is consciously distorted.

We raised the question in the previous section as to why anyone would want to deny 'the works of creation and providence' show 'the goodness, wisdom and power of God'? The answer lies in the fact that God is not only revealed as Benefactor, Architect and Governor but also as Sovereign, Legislator and Judge. The work of the law is written in our hearts, and our consciences are bearing witness to it by approving that which is good and by accusing one another and even ourselves when we sin. We know that God's requirements are righteous, but in our natural condition we love sin and want to continue in it. 'This is the condemnation, that light is come into the world, and men loved darkness rather than light, because their deeds were evil.'[16] The catalogue of evil deeds includes unrighteousness, fornication, wickedness, covetousness, maliciousness, envy, murder, debate (or strife), deceit, malignity, whispering, backbiting, hating God, being despiteful, pride, boasting, inventing evil things, being disobedient to parents, being without understanding, covenant-breaking, being without natural affection, being implacable and unmerciful.[17]

---

[16] John 3.19.

[17] See Romans 1.29–31.

## *Continuing* in Sins Makes us More Inexcusable.

Now whatever *we* might say, we know that God's judicial reaction to such deeds is to condemn them and we already have awareness that the wages of sin is death. So Paul characterizes the Gentiles in all of their depraved abandonment to sin as those *knowing the judgement of God, that they which commit such things are worthy of death.* Any frank admission on our part, without suppression of what we know to be the case, would lead us to confess that we know that the penalty of sin is death and that God as Judge will consign us to the most terrible penal sufferings in the world to come. What else could a morally pure God do with such wanton sinners? It is precisely because all of us have this knowledge that the continuation in sin is so grave. Even though we apprehend that God is Lawgiver and Judge and that his commandments are righteous and our ways, by nature, evil, yet sinners continue in these sins and approve them in others! They *not only do the same, but have pleasure in them that do them.* The whole civilization approves a manner of life which is at variance with the moral excellence of God, notwithstanding the inner knowledge that God will not ignore this flagrant disregard of His law, which renders everyone of us in our natural condition *worthy of death.* Instead of taking the path of love in saying to sinners, young and old, 'Do not ruin yourselves', our society approves what it knows to be worthy of damnation.

## *Condemning* Ourselves Shows that we are Inexcusable.

There are many religious people who would exclude themselves from the sins that Paul lists. They might say, 'I have not been a fornicator, I have not been a murderer, I have always, or nearly always, kept my word' and so on. The Jews of Paul's day were like that and looked down on the Gentiles for their gross evils. Paul himself had been self-righteous and knew what it was to judge others for the life that they lived. But here is the point; the man who condemns others is guilty of the same things! Paul goes on to say: 'thou that preachest a man should not steal, dost thou steal? Thou that sayest a man should not commit adultery, dost thou commit adultery? thou that abhorrest idols, dost thou commit sacrilege?

Thou that makest thy boast of the law, through breaking the law dishonourest thou God?'[18]

How many have turned away from religion as a result of the hypocrisy of those who professed it? There is one who sings in the choir, but he overstates his overtime claim. There is a vicar who runs off with a parishioner's wife. There are ornaments on the churchwarden's mantelpiece that were stolen from an idol temple he visited on holiday. Those who are self-righteous have only to look around their homes, read their own diaries or review their relationships with others to find plenty of examples of doing those things, which they ought not to have done. The conclusion is inescapable. We condemn ourselves in judging others because we are not free of the same things. Just under the veneer of a respectable life are many transgressions. Each must face up to the fact that by nature he is inexcusable too! This was the point that Paul had to come to before he could be saved. 'To put it bluntly, we are not only bent on damning ourselves but we congratulate others in the doing of those things that we know have their issue in damnation. We hate others as we hate ourselves and render therefore to them the approval of what we know merits damnation. Iniquity is most aggravated when it meets with no inhibition from the disapproval of others and when there is collective, undissenting approbation.'[19]

## GENERAL REVELATION IS NOT SUFFICIENT TO GIVE SAVING KNOWLEDGE

### 1 Corinthians 1.21

'For after that in the wisdom of God the world by wisdom knew not God, it pleased God by the foolishness of preaching to save them that believe.'

It has always been the confidence of the learned that, if there is a human predicament, human reasoning will be able to resolve it without reference to Christianity and the Bible. So the Deists imagined that the revelation of God the Creator was sufficient to develop a system of belief

---

[18] Romans 2.21b–23.

[19] John Murray, *op. cit.*, p.53.

whereby eternal happiness could be secured. There was nothing new in this. Long before, Greeks and others had supreme confidence in their philosophies. The confessional statement that 'the light of nature and the works of creation and providence' are 'not sufficient to give that knowledge of God and of His will which is necessary unto salvation' is thoroughly scriptural. In his first letter to the Corinthians Paul addressed this subject by making the following points: (1) God has *discarded* worldly wisdom, (2) God *destroys* worldly wisdom, and (3) God has *determined* where true wisdom will be found.

## God has *Discarded* Worldly Wisdom

First century Corinth had much in common with our contemporary world and in particular the view that human wisdom and knowledge will be enough to see us through the problems of life. The opinions of experts are the media's daily fare. It was the same in ancient Greece. Luke tells us that 'all the Athenians and strangers which were there spent their time in nothing else, but either to tell, or to hear some new thing.'[20] Paul tells us that with respect to the answer to the question, 'What must I do to be saved?'[21] this human learning is absolutely bankrupt. However relevant our natural wisdom might be in its place for commerce, navigation, technology and so on; with respect to spiritual salvation it has zero contribution. It is not wisdom but foolishness! 'Where is the wise? where is the scribe? where is the disputer of this world? hath not God made foolish the wisdom of this world?'[22] It is as though Paul would say, 'Had I lived four thousand years, with perfect liberty to explore the entire creation, probe its mysteries and accumulate the knowledge of centuries, where would I be?' 'Having no hope, and without God in the world.'[23]

No amount of rational theorizing must be allowed to dilute the plain force of the apostle's words with respect to the much-acclaimed wisdom of this world. It can save no one, and God has given to it no role in the matter of saving sinners. Charles Hodge explains the Apostle's argument at this

---

[20] Acts 17.21.

[21] Acts 16.30.

[22] 1 Corinthians 1.20.

[23] Ephesians 2.12.

point: 'experience having shown the insufficiency of human wisdom, God set it aside, and declared it to be worthless, by adopting the foolishness of preaching as the means of salvation. The argument therefore includes two distinct proofs. First, that derived from experience; and secondly that derived from God's having appointed the gospel, as distinguished from human wisdom, to be the means of saving men.'[24]

## God *Destroys* Worldly Wisdom

Far from having something to contribute it is clear that, as soon as natural wisdom sets up in competition with the Gospel of Christ in the matter of where true happiness is to be found, it has become God's enemy. When it seeks to rise above its station in this way, the most refined human learning is on course for destruction. It is God's plan to show that it can do nothing about man's spiritual plight and must utterly fail. 'For it is written, I will destroy the wisdom of the wise, and will bring to nothing the understanding of the prudent.'[25] This is true with respect to individuals. No amount of counselling will solve the deep personal needs that can only be met by Jesus Christ. It is also true with respect to society. Social policies and political action cannot get to the root of our predicament and provide a solution to the natural depravity that afflicts us all. The agencies of the state can restrain evil but they cannot eradicate it. Each passing year witnesses to the fact that strategic, economic and social policies can never be a substitute for the Gospel and that it was a fearfully wrong course that was taken when Western Society came to the conclusion that it had outgrown the need for the Gospel of Jesus Christ. This was to adopt a disaster course and each step on that disaster course brings society nearer to the destruction of its whole philosophy of life in some grand catastrophe. Thus our contemporary social decay witnesses to the need for something beyond natural religion.

A. A. Hodge maintains that it is proved that the knowledge attainable by the light of nature is insufficient for salvation:

---

[24] Charles Hodge, *A Commentary on the First Epistle to the Corinthians* (Edinburgh: The Banner of Truth Trust, 1964) p. 20.

[25] 1 Corinthians 1.19.

'From the fact that man's moral relations to God have been disturbed by sin; and while the natural light of reason may teach an unfallen being spontaneously how he should approach and serve God, and while it may teach a fallen being what the nature of God may demand as to the punishment of sin, it can teach nothing by way of anticipation as to what God may be sovereignly disposed to do in the way of remission, substitution, sanctification, restoration, etc.'

And:

'From the facts presented in the past history of all nations destitute of the light of revelation, both before and since Christ. The truths they have held have been incomplete, and mixed with fundamental error; their faith has been uncertain; their religious rites have been degrading, and their lives immoral.'[26]

## God has *Determined* Where True Wisdom will be Found

The failure of human philosophy is not accidental. It arises from the Divine purpose. God never intended that natural religion would save the world. Exactly the opposite is true. God intended to demonstrate the failure of the wisdom of this world in spiritual things, despite its undoubted accomplishments, so that his method of saving sinners would have no legitimate competitor. Despite being surrounded by all of the manifestations of the Divine glory in creation and providence none have come to a saving knowledge of God through the consideration of this revelation. *For after that in the wisdom of God the world by wisdom knew not God, it pleased God by the foolishness of preaching to save them that believe.* Paul goes on to demonstrate that the message that sinners reject is their only hope of salvation. 'For the Jews require a sign, and the Greeks seek after wisdom: But we preach Christ crucified, unto the Jews a stumblingblock, and unto the Greeks foolishness; But unto

---

[26] A. A. Hodge, *The Confession of Faith: A Handbook of Christian Doctrine Expounding The Westminster Confession* (Edinburgh: The Banner of Truth Trust, 1964) p. 28.

them which are called, both Jews and Greeks, Christ the power of God,
and the wisdom of God.'[27]

### *1 Corinthians 2.13–14*

'Which things also we speak, not in the words which man's
wisdom teacheth, but which the Holy Ghost teacheth;
comparing spiritual things with spiritual. But the natural
man receiveth not the things of the Spirit of God: for they
are foolishness unto him: neither can he know them,
because they are spiritually discerned.'

In these verses Paul excludes any prospect of saving knowledge by
means of General Revelation by showing that his message was God-
given, that it was communicated by reference to Spirit-taught words, as
opposed to the words of man's wisdom, and that spiritual enlightenment
is essential in order to understand the things of God. We will consider
(1) The *Source* of the message of salvation, (2) The *Spirit-taught words*
by which the message of salvation is communicated and (3) The *spiritual
enlightenment* needed to receive the message of salvation.

### The *Source* of the Message of Salvation

The things of which the apostle speaks are 'the things of God' which he
'revealed' to Paul 'by His Spirit.'[28] These things cannot be discovered by
human reason. The 'princes of this world' did not know 'the wisdom of
God'.[29] No other man can know our secret thoughts. If this is true of
humans, how much more must it be the case that no man can know the
inner thoughts of God? 'For what man knoweth the things of a man, save
the spirit of man which is in him? even so the things of God knoweth no
man, but the Spirit of God.'[30] God must reveal what originates in God.

---

[27] 1 Corinthians 1.22–24.

[28] 1 Corinthians 2.10–11.

[29] 1 Corinthians 2.8,7.

[30] 1 Corinthians 2.11.

## The *Spirit-taught Words* by which the Message of Salvation is Communicated

The apostle makes plain that he did not even resort to the learning of men in order to find the best words in which to communicate the message of salvation. Paul preached a message revealed by the Spirit of God; and he communicated these spiritual things in an appropriate spiritual way using Spirit-taught words. *Which things also we speak, not in the words which man's wisdom teacheth, but which the Holy Ghost teacheth; comparing spiritual things with spiritual.* The wisdom of men could not be more effectively shut out. It had no place. Paul's message did not originate in human reason and neither did the words that he used to proclaim it. The word's of man's wisdom have nothing to contribute to the preaching of the Gospel and would detract from it. 'My speech and my preaching was not with enticing words of man's wisdom, but in demonstration of the Spirit and of power. That your faith should not stand in the wisdom of men, but in the power of God.'[31]

## The *Spiritual Enlightenment* Needed to Receive the Message of Salvation

So far is anyone from being able to arrive at a saving knowledge of God from the light of nature and the consideration of the works of creation and providence, that he or she cannot even understand the things of the Spirit of God when presented with them! *The natural man receiveth not the things of the Spirit of God: for they are foolishness unto him.* Despite the clarity of the message and the inspired words in which the apostles communicated it, in our natural condition we just do not understand it. To the unrenewed person the Gospel is both absurd and distasteful. It is not that the Gospel is not true, authoritative and excellent. It is that without the regenerating power of the Holy Spirit the natural man is incapable of understanding the things of God *neither can he know them, because they are spiritually discerned.* An inward change of heart is needed so that the beauty and power of the Gospel message can be appreciated and apprehended. All progress in understanding God's salvation necessitates spiritual enlightenment.

---

[31] 1 Corinthians 2.4–5.

# Chapter 2

## *The Necessity Of Scripture: A Permanent Revelation*

*Redemptive Revelation – The Purposed Benefits of Written Revelation –
The Necessity of the Holy Scriptures*

### REDEMPTIVE REVELATION

We have seen in the previous chapter that the *Westminster Confession of Faith* states:

> 'Although the light of nature and the works of creation and providence do so far manifest the goodness, wisdom and power of God, as to leave men unexcusable; yet are they not sufficient to give that knowledge of God and of His will, which is necessary unto salvation. Therefore it pleased the Lord, at sundry times, and in divers manners, to reveal Himself, and to declare that His will unto His Church; and afterwards, for the better preserving and propagating of the truth, and for the more sure establishment and comfort of the Church against the corruption of the flesh, and the malice of Satan and of the world, to commit the same wholly unto writing; which maketh the Holy Scripture to be most necessary; those former ways of God's revealing His will unto His people being now ceased.'[1]

The first part of this paragraph was considered in *Chapter 1* and we have seen that the need for the Scripture arises because the revelation of God the Creator cannot save sinners. God is made known to us by the light of nature and by the works of creation and providence and these reveal the

---

[1] 'The Confession of Faith of the Westminster Assembly of Divines' Chapter 1.1 in S. W. Carruthers (ed.), *The Westminster Confession of Faith* (Manchester: R. Aikman & Son, 1937) p. 89.

goodness, wisdom and power of God leaving even the heathen without excuse if they do not worship the Creator. However, this revelation does not make God known to us as Redeemer and the revelation of God the Creator cannot save sinners. It is for this reason that God has revealed Himself as Saviour in a variety of ways to his Church. The need for the Bible arises because the preservation and proclamation of saving truth in the face of the attacks of the world, the flesh and the Devil is better served by a written revelation. The scriptures thus provide for the comfort of the Church against the flesh, the malice of Satan, and the malice of the world. The need for the Scripture is the greater because the former fragmentary revelations of the way of salvation have now ceased.

*Hebrews 1.1*

'God, who at sundry times and in divers manners spake in time past unto the fathers by the prophets...'

The testimony of Christianity is that God has spoken 'to reveal himself, and to declare... His will unto His Church.' The *necessity* of this redemptive revelation is considered here and the *nature* of the ancient redemptive revelation. We can thus see the relation of the latter to both general revelation and written redemptive revelation.

### The *Necessity* of Redemptive Revelation

Literature that appeals neither to idle curiosity by fanciful tales nor to lust with filthy licentiousness needs some commendation to people today. Medical self-help manuals might not be best sellers but if they supply answers to chronic ailments those who are aware of their sickness will read them. The revelation of God the Creator is 'not sufficient to give that knowledge of God, and of His will, which is necessary unto salvation', but it is sufficient to leave us inexcusable. Our problem as sinners is plain but the remedy is not everywhere apparent. But God has revealed himself as Redeemer, in a variety of ways in ancient times.

### The *Nature* of the Ancient Redemptive Revelation

In former ages *at sundry times and in divers manners* God spoke to *the fathers by the prophets.* The Originator of what the prophets had to say was God. The ancient prophecies were not men's ideas about the way of salvation. The revelation came from God. It was gradually imparted over centuries in different portions by theophanies (Divine appearances), audible voices, typical persons and actions, dreams, visions, the Urim and Thummim, emblematic actions, laws, parables, songs and prophecies. John Brown is careful to distinguish the modes of revelation to the prophets from the ways in which the prophets revealed the message to the fathers. He states: 'the Apostle is not speaking of the variety of the modes of revelation, as made to the prophets, but as made by them to the fathers. The revelation was sometimes communicated by typical representations and emblematical actions, sometimes in a continued parable, at other times by separate figures, at other times – though comparatively rarely – in plain explicit language.'[2] Despite the different times and methods, the same way of salvation was revealed as God expanded that first statement of it to the serpent: 'And I will put enmity between thee and the woman, and between thy seed and her seed; it shall bruise thy head, and thou shalt bruise his heel.'[3]

## THE PURPOSED BENEFITS OF WRITTEN REVELATION

*Proverbs 22.19–21*

> 'That thy trust may be in the Lord, I have made known to thee this day, even to thee. Have not I written to thee excellent things in counsels and knowledge, That I might make thee know the certainty of the words of truth; that thou mightest answer the words of truth to them that send unto thee?'

God had a purpose in giving his Word in written form as Holy Scripture and it is our duty to consider the intended benefits so that we do profit from them. We may mention: (1) the *preservation* of the truth, (2) the *perseverance* of the saints and (3) the *proclamation* of God's Word.

---

[2] John Brown, *An Exposition of the Epistle to the Hebrews* (Edinburgh: The Banner of Truth Trust, 1964) p. 19.

[3] Genesis 3.15.

## The *Preservation* of the Truth

Proverbs 22.19–21 emphasizes the written Word: *Have not I written to thee excellent things in counsels and knowledge.* Godly teachers were often commanded to write. 'The Lord said unto Moses, Write thou these words: for after the tenor of these words I have made a covenant with thee and with Israel.'[4] The Lord commanded Jeremiah: 'Take thee a roll of a book, and write therein all the words that I have spoken unto thee...'[5] When Jehoiakim burnt the scroll, the word of the Lord came to Jeremiah saying: 'Take thee again another roll, and write in it all the former words that were in the first roll, which Jehoiakim the king of Judah hath burned.'[6] We have here one of the clearest examples of the Divine intention to preserve the Word of God in permanent written form against all despisers and attackers so that heavenly wisdom might be preserved on earth.

## The *Perseverance* of the Saints

The 'establishment and comfort of the Church' is near to God's heart. He loves his people and would have them to know him and his ways. *That thy trust may be in the Lord, I have made known to thee this day, even to thee. ...That I might make thee know the certainty of the words of truth.* Victorious trust arises from sound knowledge, and reliable knowledge of Divine things is obtained from Scripture. The faith that takes this route to wisdom will be a triumphant faith because God's Word written can be relied upon. So Bridges urges: 'But let us not forget the great end of this Revelation – *that we may know the certainty of the things;* that *we may give an answer* concerning our confidence.'[7]

## The *Proclamation* of God's Word

According to the Apostle Paul, heart and mouth go together. 'For with the heart man believeth unto righteousness; and with the mouth

---

[4] Exodus 34.27.

[5] Jeremiah 36.2.

[6] Jeremiah 36.28.

[7] Charles Bridges, *A Commentary on Proverbs* (Edinburgh: The Banner of Truth Trust, 1968) pp. 417–418.

confession is made unto salvation.'[8] In this connection our testimony is not to depend upon uncertain memory or the speculative opinions of men but is to depend upon objective, propositional, recorded revelation:

*Have not I written to thee excellent things in counsels and knowledge... that thou mightest answer the words of truth to them that send unto thee?*

## The Establishment of the Church

### Luke 1.1–4

'Forasmuch as many have taken in hand to set forth in order a declaration of those things which are most surely believed among us, Even as they delivered them unto us, which from the beginning were eyewitnesses, and ministers of the word; It seemed good to me also, having had perfect understanding of all things from the very first, to write unto thee in order, most excellent Theophilus, That thou mightest know the certainty of those things, wherein thou hast been instructed.'

Luke is concerned about the establishment of the Church. He wants his readers to understand that he has written his Gospel for 'the establishment' of God's people. A written record makes this 'more sure' than what would be attained by reliance upon memory and oral accounts. He has written so that Theophilus and others might *know the certainty of those things* in which they had been instructed. The time would come when eyewitness testimony would no longer be available, although it was by such oral witness that the truth was initially delivered to the church. The things *most surely believed* were *delivered* by those who *from the beginning were eyewitnesses, and ministers of the word.* Geldenhuys explains that the expression 'refers to the apostles, who were all eyewitnesses of Jesus, and the first reliable preachers of the glad tidings. Luke, therefore, lays special emphasis on the fact that those writings are by no means the collecting of mere legends or human gossip, but the written rendering of what had really happened and had been communicated by authoritative witnesses. Here, therefore, we have

---

[8] Romans 10.10.

to deal not with fabricated fables but with the written reproduction of the tradition of the apostles.'[9] The Apostle John also used written communication to ensure that believers would have a joyous assurance: 'That which was from the beginning, which we have heard, which we have seen with our eyes, which we have looked upon, and our hands have handled, of the Word of life; (For the life was manifested, and we have seen it, and bear witness, and shew unto you that eternal life, which was with the Father, and was manifested unto us;) That which we have seen and heard declare we unto you, that ye also may have fellowship with us: and truly our fellowship is with the Father, and with his Son Jesus Christ. And these things write we unto you, that your joy may be full.'[10] Such witness on the basis of eyewitness evidence was to be an unrepeated experience. There could be no future oral eyewitness testimony to the life, teaching, prayers, miracles, sufferings and death of Jesus Christ once the generation of the 'days of his flesh'[11] had passed away. Such witness cannot be repeated. Christ lived in the first century and only those alive then could witness to what they had seen.

Therefore, in his infinite wisdom and mercy, God inspired men like John and Luke *to write* concerning the Saviour so that there might be a *New Testament* counterpart to the *Old Testament* witness to the Messiah in the Jewish Scriptures. Luke refers to previous writings emphasizing that the basis of the written records was the eyewitness testimony.[12] Scriptures of this quality of evidence could be delivered only once, and in the first century, before the *eyewitnesses* died. All of the books of the New Testament issued from this eyewitness context. This was true of Paul who had not only seen the risen Lord, but who laboured among those who were eyewitnesses and apostles and to whom Paul's doctrine and writings were familiar.[13] Never again could these conditions for an authoritative written record witnessing to the life, death and resurrection

---

[9] Norval Geldenhuys, *Commentary on the Gospel of Luke: The English Text with Introduction Exposition and Notes* (Grand Rapids: Wm. B. Eerdmans Publishing Company, 1975) p.52.

[10] 1 John 1.1–4.

[11] Hebrews 5.7.

[12] Luke 1.2.

[13] Acts 9.1–7, Acts 15, Galatians 1.15–2.16 and 2 Peter 3.15–16.

of Christ be fulfilled. Luke might have said to himself: 'It is now or never!' Never again could any supposed revelation claim to have such an eyewitness context concerning Christ in his life, death and resurrection like that of the authentic New Testament Scriptures. The circumstances will never be reproduced. Revelation such as exists in the New Testament is unique. Luke's Gospel partakes of this uniqueness and Luke himself tells us that he pursued his work with thoroughness and care to write an orderly and connected narrative providing a reasonably comprehensive and utterly reliable record. The Greek translated *in order* includes logical order as well as chronological order. Luke is not limiting himself to time sequence but he is being systematic. Theophilus had apparently already received some instruction in the truth but Luke writes for him and others like him so that they might have a sure knowledge of the unshakeable historical facts upon which the Christian Faith rests and the spiritual significance of those facts. Spirit-wrought faith thus founded results in an establishment in the truth that is invincible against the world, the flesh and the Devil.

## The Comfort of Believers Despite the Corruption of the Flesh

### *Romans 15.4*

'For whatsoever things were written aforetime were written
for our learning, that we through patience and comfort of
the scriptures might have hope.'

To be without hope is a most miserable condition. Such is the plight of the hungry, thirsty, lonely wanderer who is homeless and fainting. The prisoner manacled in his dark cell awaiting execution falls down under the burden of his helplessness. The terminally sick who not only do not desire food but abhor it are in a desperate case. The brave sailor caught in a great storm is tossed to and fro and staggers like a drunkard until all courage fails and he is at his wit's end expecting total loss of cargo, ship and life.[14] Oh to have comfort, to find a dwelling place, to be set free, to be recovered and to have a safe haven! Such is God's provision for those who trust him. 'Then they cried unto the Lord in their trouble, and he

---

[14] Psalm 107.1–27.

delivered them out of their distresses.'[15] There is a resort to him who has revealed himself in the Scriptures. The action of the Word of God *written* is of mighty effect in every time of need and every sort of need. The frequency of the appeal to the Old Testament Scriptures by the New Testament writers shows their conviction that God had given his Word in written form for the express purpose of answering to life's greatest needs. 'For whatsoever things were written aforetime were written for our learning, *that we through patience and comfort of the scriptures might have hope.*' They impart to us instruction for our learning, in order that, empowered for patient endurance with respect to every affliction and comforted and consoled, we might not despair but have a robust hope in God. Professor John Murray comments: 'Both the stedfastness and the comfort are derived from the Scriptures and are, therefore, dependent upon these Scriptures and draw their character and value from them. These are generated by Scripture and their quality is determined by Scripture. However, the stedfastness and consolation are said to be the means of something more ultimate, namely, hope.'[16]

## The Overthrow of the Malice of Satan

### Matthew 4.4,7,10

'But he answered and said, It is written, Man shall not live by bread alone, but by every word that proceedeth out of the mouth of God... Jesus said unto him, It is written again, Thou shalt not tempt the Lord thy God... Then saith Jesus unto him, Get thee hence, Satan: for it is written, Thou shalt worship the Lord thy God, and him only shalt thou serve.'

The Lord himself sets the example of the overthrow of Satan by the written Word. It was *Jesus* who *said unto him, It is written again, Thou shalt not tempt the Lord thy God.* It is not just that Jesus used the written Word of God to repel the temptations of the Devil;[17] he specifically

---

[15] Psalm 107.6.

[16] John Murray, *The Epistle to the Romans: The English Text with Introduction Exposition and Notes,* Volume II (Grand Rapids: Wm. B. Eerdmans Publishing Company, 1975) p. 200.

[17] *Diabolos*, the Slanderer.

draws attention to the fact that this is his method so that the authority of the Scriptures for this purpose might be recognized by his assailant and by his disciples. Three times he uses the perfect passive indicative of the Greek verb 'I write' meaning 'it has been written and remains so.' The writing was completed in the past and stands as the final authority on the matter. It must have the last word. God has 'spoken'[18]. Against this word Satan, 'the Adversary', cannot stand. 'Then saith Jesus unto him, *Get thee hence, Satan*: for it is written, Thou shalt worship the Lord thy God, and him only shalt thou serve.' This power to dispatch Satan is in the authoritative Word of God, whether in the hand of Christ or the weakest saint. The power remains in what is *written,* irrespective of the weakness of the one who uses the Word. It served for the perfect Christ and it serves for imperfect saints. The Scriptures as the God-breathed word are the source of our life in the deepest and fullest sense for 'it is written, Man shall not live by bread alone, *but by every word that proceedeth out of the mouth of God.'*[19]

## Victory Over the World

### Isaiah 8.19–20

'And when they shall say unto you, Seek unto them that have familiar spirits, and unto wizards that peep, and that mutter: should not a people seek unto their God? for the living to the dead? To the law and to the testimony: if they speak not according to this word, it is because there is no light in them.'

It is God who gives the precedence to his revelation of himself, which he was pleased to 'commit' to 'writing'. God's people are tempted by others to seek guidance in the ways 'of the world'. At its most extreme this

---

[18] Hebrews 1.2.

[19] Note the helpful comment: 'What the Scripture speaks indifferently to all is to be esteemed as spoken to every singular person, and the singular persons are to be accounted as addressed in the writing of the general: for upon this ground Christ says, *It is written* again, Thou shalt not tempt the Lord thy God, because in Deuteronomy 6.16 it is written, *Ye shall not tempt the Lord your God.*' David Dickson, *A Brief Exposition of the Evangel of Jesus Christ According to Matthew* (Edinburgh: The Banner of Truth Trust, 1981) p. 37.

involves looking to *them that have familiar spirits, and unto wizards that peep, and that mutter.* Those *that have familiar spirits* are 'those possessing the spirit of witchcraft' where the dead are supposed to speak. *Wizards* are supposedly 'knowing' and wise because possessing a soothsaying spirit; and using chirping noises purporting to be the noise of underworld bats. God commands his people to seek him where he may be found, in his written Word, saying: *to the law and to the testimony.* All of the people of God are competent to resort to this rule, which from its inception became the standard to determine the nature of supposed revelations. *If they speak not according to this word, it is because there is no light in them.* No prophetic gifts are needed in order to distinguish light from darkness because the scriptures are our sufficiency. Those who would live by another guide remain in their corruption and now and in the future will not see the light of the everlasting day. It is of believers that Peter can say: 'We have also a more sure word of prophecy; whereunto ye do well that ye take heed, as unto a light that shineth in a dark place, until the day dawn, and the day star arise in your hearts...'[20]

## THE NECESSITY OF THE HOLY SCRIPTURES

The Word of God written is necessary because: (1) the Scriptures are the *repository* of saving truth, (2) the Scriptures are to be *resorted* to for saving truth and (3) the scriptures are *THE revelation* of saving truth as former methods of revelation have now ceased.

### The Scriptures are the *Repository* of Saving Truth

#### 2 Timothy 3.15

> 'And that from a child thou hast known the holy scriptures,
> which are able to make thee wise unto salvation through
> faith which is in Christ Jesus.'

The word of God written is Holy Scripture. Paul refers to the *holy scriptures* or 'sacred writings'. We use the words *writing* and *script* when we refer to handwriting. In 2 Corinthians 3.6 Paul uses the same word for 'letters' of the alphabet. *Scripture* is thus a very exact word to

---

[20] 2 Peter 1.19.

use to translate the original Greek. Timothy had early exposure to the Old Testament and this was of great advantage to him because the *scriptures* have the power to make us *wise unto salvation.* In order to have heavenly wisdom the scriptures must be believed. They make wise to salvation *through faith which is in Christ Jesus.* There is now no other source of such redemptive revelation, God having appointed his written word expressly for the purpose of giving that instruction which is to life eternal.

**The Scriptures are to be *Resorted to* for Saving Truth**

*2 Peter 1.19*

> 'We have also a more sure word of prophecy; whereunto ye do well that ye take heed, as unto a light that shineth in a dark place, until the day dawn, and the day star arise in your hearts...'

Peter pays tribute to the scriptures when he refers to them as *a more sure word of prophecy* than God himself speaking audibly from Heaven.[21] We cannot imagine any kind of spoken revelation now that could rival such a miracle. But as to enduring accessibility, the Bible excels such revelation because of its permanence of form. This written word of God is now a more sure confirmation of his will than the voice that Peter heard because it remains with us. It has the excellence of the letter over the telephone conversation. We can return to the letter again and again to confirm precisely what was said. There is none of the weakness of relying upon our memory or the memory of others. The scriptures are thus indispensable and are commended to us for our attention in the command *whereunto ye do well that ye take heed.* If we would have light we must seek it in this *light that shineth in a dark place* or we will continue in the darkness of sin and stumble and fall irretrievably. There is an urgency about the necessity of Holy Scripture that we must not overlook.

---

[21] 2 Peter 1.17–18.

**The Scriptures are *THE Revelation* of Saving Truth as Former Methods of Revelation have Now Ceased**

*Hebrews 1.1–2*

'God, who at sundry times and in divers manners spake in time past unto the fathers by the prophets, Hath in these last days spoken unto us by his Son, whom he hath appointed heir of all things, by whom also he made the worlds...'

There is a finality about the revelation in the Bible; the 'former ways of God's revealing His will unto His people being now ceased.' There were other methods of God making himself known but these have been replaced. *God, who... spake in time past unto the fathers by the prophets, Hath in these last days spoken unto us by his Son.* The keynote of the superiority of Christianity over Judaism, which runs through the Epistle to the Hebrews, starts in the opening words in connection with revelation. The former *method* of revelation is replaced. It has served its purpose. The *content* remains valid but the ancient revelation was preparatory, incomplete, obscure and progressing. It has now found its fulfilment in Jesus Christ, the eternal Son come in the flesh. The record concerning Him contains the fulfilment of the prophets; it is complete, clear and final. Further revelation is superfluous. In sum:

The prophets have reached their pinnacle in the Son.

The preparation has come to its fulfillment.

The partial has been completed.

The obscure has been illuminated by the clear.

The progressing has reached its finalization.

Arthur Pink draws attention to the threefold contrast between God's communications through Judaism and Christianity: 'First, in their respective *characters*: the one was fragmentary and incomplete; the other perfect and final. Second, in the *instruments* which He employed: in the former, it was sinful men; in the latter, His holy Son. Third, in the *periods* selected: the one was "in time past," the other in "these last days," intimating that God has now fully expressed Himself, that He has nothing in reserve.'[22]

---

[22] Arthur W. Pink, *An Exposition of Hebrews* (Grand Rapids: Baker Book House, 1954) p. 25.

# Chapter 3

## *The Canon Of Scripture*

*The Concept of the Canon – The Divisions of the Scriptures – The Formation of the Canon*

Paragraphs 2 and 3 of the *Westminster Confession of Faith* deal with the important subject of the definition of Scripture. What books are we talking about when we refer to the scriptures or Holy Scripture? The Confession provides us with a definition.

> '2. Under the name of Holy Scripture, or the Word of God written, are now contained all the books of the Old and New Testament, which are these: Of the Old Testament: *Genesis, Exodus, Leviticus, Numbers, Deuteronomy, Joshua, Judges, Ruth, I Samuel, II Samuel, I Kings, II Kings, I Chronicles, II Chronicles, Ezra, Nehemiah, Esther, Job, Psalms, Proverbs, Ecclesiastes, The Song of Songs, Isaiah, Jeremiah, Lamentations, Ezekiel, Daniel, Hosea, Joel, Amos, Obadiah, Jonah, Micah, Nahum, Habakkuk, Zephaniah, Haggai, Zechariah, Malachi.* Of the New Testament: *The Gospels according to Matthew, Mark, Luke, John; The Acts of the Apostles; Paul's Epistles: To the Romans, Corinthians I, Corinthians II, Galatians, Ephesians, Philippians, Colossians, Thessalonians I, Thessalonians II, To Timothy I, To Timothy II, To Titus, To Philemon, The Epistle to the Hebrews; The Epistle of James; The first and second Epistles of Peter; The first, second, and third Epistles of John; The Epistle of Jude; The Revelation of John.* All which are given by inspiration of God, to be the rule of faith and life.'[1]

> '3. The books commonly called Apocrypha, not being of divine inspiration, are no part of the canon of the Scripture;

---

[1] Luke 16:29,31; Ephesians 2:20; Revelation 22:18,19; 2 Timothy 3:16.

and therefore are of no authority in the Church of God, nor to be any otherwise approved, or made use of, than other human writings.'[2]

In Warfield's analysis these two paragraphs provide the Definition of Scripture as follows:

(a) *Extensively*: The Canon, S. 2a.

(b) *Intensively*: Inspiration, S. 2b.

(c) *Exclusively*: The Apocrypha, S. 3.[3]

In this chapter we consider the first of these, the Canon of Scripture and in the following chapter we will consider Inspiration and the Apocrypha.

## THE CONCEPT OF THE CANON

Our English word 'canon' is derived through the Greek from the ancient Hebrew. In the prophecy of Ezekiel reference is made to a measuring reed (*qaneh*). When the idea of 'that which measures' is applied to human behaviour it is thought of as a *rule* that governs actions. As such it could be used to refer to a summary of teachings that set the standard of faith and practice. When applied to the Bible '*The Canon*' indicated the list of books included in the collection known as Scripture and recognised by the Church as possessing Divine authority as the rule of faith and practice. The Bible contains sixty-six books. The name *Bible* reflects this. It is derived through Latin from the Greek word *biblia* meaning 'books'. The scriptures are a collection of books. The description is a biblical one. 'In the first year of his reign I Daniel understood *by books* the number of the years, whereof the word of the Lord came to Jeremiah the prophet, that he would accomplish seventy years in the desolations of Jerusalem.'[4]

---

[2] Proof texts: Luke 24:27,44; Romans 3:2; 2 Peter 1:21. 'The Confession of Faith of the Westminster Assembly of Divines' Chapter 1.2 in S. W. Carruthers (ed.), *The Westminster Confession of Faith* (Manchester: R. Aikman & Son, 1937) p. 90.

[3] B. B. Warfield, *The Westminster Assembly and its Work, Volume VI* (Grand Rapids: Baker Book House, 1991) p.191.

[4] Daniel 9:2.

The earliest surviving reference in the early church is about AD 150 in 2 Clement 14.2: 'the books and the apostles declare that the Church... has existed from the beginning.' The expression 'Books' is still used in Scotland. When we have in our hands the Bible, *what* we are holding is a divinely inspired library. We must ask ourselves the question: How often do we go to the library? Is it once a week or once a month? With this library it must be every day. Every library has a catalogue so that you can find your way around. There has to be some order or classification that relates to the contents of the books. With respect to this divine library we need to consider the twofold division, the threefold division and the fivefold division.

## THE DIVISIONS OF THE SCRIPTURES

In this section we will consider (1) The Twofold Division of the Scriptures, (2) The Threefold Division of the Old Testament and (3) The Fivefold Division of the Law. In closing this section we will look at the Fivefold Grouping of the New Testament Books in the Westminster Confession.

### The Twofold Division of the Scriptures

*2 Corinthians 3.14–15*

> 'But their minds were blinded: for until this day remaineth the same vail untaken away in the reading of the old testament; which vail is done away in Christ. But even unto this day, when Moses is read, the vail is upon their heart.'

The Bible divides into the Old Testament and the New Testament. This is a biblical division. Paul applies the former description to the books of Moses, the foundation of the Old Testament: 'But their minds were blinded: for until this day remaineth the same vail untaken away *in the reading of the old testament...*' Christ spoke of the New Testament in the words of the institution of the Lord's Supper: 'Likewise also the cup after supper, saying, This cup is the *new testament* in my blood, which is shed for you.'[5] This terminology points to the central feature of salvation,

---

[5] Luke 22.20.

43

namely, that all saving experience stems from God's covenant of grace. Paul explains this to the Galatians as follows. 'Now to Abraham and his seed were the promises made. He saith not, And to seeds, as of many; but as of one, And to thy seed, which is Christ. And this I say, that the covenant, that was confirmed before of God in Christ, the law, which was four hundred and thirty years after, cannot disannul, that it should make the promise of none effect. For if the inheritance be of the law, it is no more of promise: but God gave it to Abraham by promise.'[6]

The covenant is God's sovereign arrangement or disposition.[7] It is a gracious covenant. It stems from his undeserved kindness. It is confirmed in Christ for he is the exclusive mediator of the covenant. This covenant bestows an inheritance upon undeserving sinners. It is a covenant of promise and all of its benefits are received by faith. It is not inappropriate to think of a 'testament'. This is a more specific illustration and helps us to see that God, like a testator of a will is sovereign in bestowing an inheritance upon his beneficiaries. 'And for this cause he is the mediator of the new testament, that by means of death, for the redemption of the transgressions that were under the first testament, they which are called might receive the promise of eternal inheritance. For where a testament is, there must also of necessity be the death of the testator. For a testament is of force after men are dead: otherwise it is of no strength at all while the testator liveth. Whereupon neither the first testament was dedicated without blood. For when Moses had spoken every precept to all the people according to the law, he took the blood of calves and of goats, with water, and scarlet wool, and hyssop, and sprinkled both the book, and all the people, Saying, This is the blood of the testament which God hath enjoined unto you.'[8]

---

[6] Galatians 3.16–18.

[7] Ridderbos helpfully notes: 'In LXX διαθήκη is regularly used as the translation of the covenant of God (*berith*), rather than the apparently more available word συνθήκη. In this there is already an expression of the fact that the covenant of God does not have the character of a contract between two parties, but rather that of a one-sided grant.' Herman N. Ridderbos, *The Epistle of Paul to the Churches of Galatia: The English Text with Introduction, Exposition and Notes* (Grand Rapids: Wm. B. Eerdmans Publishing Co., 1968), Footnote 2, p. 130.

[8] Hebrews 9.15–20.

There is no contradiction between the Old Testament and the New Testament. The Old Testament is not salvation by law and the New Testament salvation by grace. The Law was never intended to *save* sinners. That it can never do. The Law causes the sinner to see how much he needs to be saved by Christ. 'Wherefore the law was our schoolmaster to bring us unto Christ, that we might be justified by faith.'[9] The way of being saved by grace through faith in God's promises concerning Christ was operative before the Law. 'And this I say, that the covenant, that was confirmed before of God in Christ, the law, which was four hundred and thirty years after, cannot disannul, that it should make the promise of none effect.'[10] The way of salvation has not changed. As Thomas Taylor puts it: 'The same Testator made both Testaments.'[11] The relationship between the two is sometimes stated in the following way: 'The new is in the old concealed. The old is in the new revealed.'

## The *Threefold* Division of the Old Testament

### *Luke 24.44–47*

'And he said unto them, These are the words which I spake unto you, while I was yet with you, that all things must be fulfilled, which were written in the law of Moses, and in the prophets, and in the psalms, concerning me. Then opened he their understanding, that they might understand the scriptures, And said unto them, Thus it is written, and thus it behoved Christ to suffer, and to rise from the dead the third day: And that repentance and remission of sins should be preached in his name among all nations, beginning at Jerusalem.'

When we look at the Old Testament in the original Hebrew we are faced with a threefold division: the Law, the prophets and the writings. Christ used this description of the Old Testament: *written in the law of Moses, and in the prophets, and in the psalms, concerning me.* The 'writings' are

---

[9] Galatians 3.24.

[10] Galatians 3.17.

[11] Quoted in I. D. E. Thomas, *The Golden Treasury of Puritan Quotations* (Edinburgh: The Banner of Truth Trust, 1997) p.34.

here referred to as 'the psalms' because the Book of Psalms was the first book of the 'holy writings' in the Hebrew Bible. This teaching of Jesus shows that all parts of the Old Testament witness to Christ, his atonement and resurrection, which provide the foundation for preaching salvation to the ends of the earth through faith in him. We may not be lax about the use of the Old Testament as though its teaching is no longer relevant. It was the risen Lord himself who expounded these books to his disciples and they felt the power of their content. 'And they said one to another, Did not our heart burn within us, while he talked with us by the way, and while he opened to us the scriptures?'[12]

The Lord Jesus Christ also clearly taught that anyone who despises the authority and sufficiency of the Old Testament for salvation would not be persuaded by the most spectacular miracle. In the parable of the rich man and Lazarus, note the request of the rich man in Hell and the response of Abraham. 'Then he said, I pray thee therefore, father, that thou wouldest send him to my father's house: For I have five brethren; that he may testify unto them, lest they also come into this place of torment. Abraham saith unto him, They have Moses and the prophets; let them hear them. And he said, Nay, father Abraham: but if one went unto them from the dead, they will repent. And he said unto him, If they hear not Moses and the prophets, neither will they be persuaded, though one rose from the dead.'[13]

It will be helpful at this point if we group the books of the Old Testament into their Jewish categories and see the contents of the three divisions. We do this first of all keeping them in the order of our English Bibles to which we are accustomed and inserting the appropriate Jewish Old Testament titles. This would be as shown in *Table 3.1*.

---

[12] Luke 24.32.
[13] Luke 16.27–31.

## The Books of the Old Testament
## According to the Jewish Categories

| | |
|---|---|
| *The Law* | Genesis, Exodus, Leviticus, Numbers, Deuteronomy |
| *The Former Prophets* | Joshua, Judges |
| *The Writings* | Ruth |
| *The Former Prophets* | I Samuel, II Samuel, I Kings, II Kings |
| *The Writings* | I Chronicles, II Chronicles, Ezra, Nehemiah, Esther, Job, Psalms, Proverbs, Ecclesiastes, and The Song of Songs |
| *The Latter Prophets* | Isaiah, Jeremiah |
| *The Writings* | Lamentations |
| *The Latter Prophets* | Ezekiel |
| *The Writings* | Daniel |
| *The Twelve* | Hosea, Joel, Amos, Obadiah, Jonah, Micah, Nahum, Habakkuk, Zephaniah, Haggai, Zechariah, and Malachi |

*Table 3.1*

At this point we will take out *The Writings* and place them at the bottom of the list. We then have the books in the Jewish order: The Law, The Prophets and The Writings. In order to indicate the order of the books within The Writings each book is listed under the group to which it belongs and numbered as appropriate. In this way it is possible to clearly see how the Jewish order diverges from what we are used to in our English Bibles. This is shown in *Table 3.2.*

## The Books of the Old Testament
## as arranged in the Jewish Scriptures

| | |
|---|---|
| *The Law* | Genesis, Exodus, Leviticus, Numbers, Deuteronomy |
| *The Prophets* | |
| *The Former Prophets* | Joshua, Judges; I Samuel, II Samuel, I Kings, II Kings |
| *The Latter Prophets* | Isaiah, Jeremiah; Ezekiel; *The Twelve*: Hosea, Joel, Amos, Obadiah, Jonah, Micah, Nahum, Habakkuk, Zephaniah, Haggai, Zechariah, Malachi |

*The Writings*

| First Group | Second Group | Third Group |
|---|---|---|
| | Ruth (2.2) | |
| | | I Chronicles (3.4) |
| | | II Chronicles (3.5) |
| | | Ezra (3.2) |
| | | Nehemiah (3.3) |
| | Esther (2.5) | |
| Job (1.3) | | |
| Psalms (1.1) | | |
| Proverbs (1.2) | | |
| | Ecclesiastes(2.4) | |
| | Song of Songs (2.1) | |
| | Lamentations (2.3) | |
| | | Daniel (3.1) |

*Table 3.2*

We can see from this that the major difference of order is accounted for by *The Writings* and that the order within this category is quite different from our English Bibles: (1.1–3) Psalms, Proverbs, Job; (2.1–5) Song, Ruth, Lamentations, Ecclesiastes, Esther; (3.1–5) Daniel, Ezra, Nehemiah, I Chronicles, II Chronicles. It is presumably this grouping that accounts for the description 'the Law, the Prophets and *the Psalms*'.

What, we may ask, accounts for this arrangement? *The Law* contains the record of God's foundational work concerning Israel and his authoritative word to Israel. *The Prophets* contain the record of the historical development of Israel as a nation in the Promised Land, details of Israel's decline and Jehovah's testimony of judgment and grace. In *The Writings* we have further historical and prophetic material and poetic writings, which portray the authentic spiritual experience.

Consider *Table 3.3*, which is presented in the order in which the books appear in our English Bibles. This has been slightly modified, to show in three columns which section of the Hebrew canon contains each book. The numbers in italic type following the entries in the third column indicate the order of the books in the Hebrew Canon.

First, Psalms, Proverbs and Job, followed by the five Scrolls: Song of Solomon, Ruth, Lamentations, Ecclesiastes and Esther. The canon closes with Daniel, Ezra, Nehemiah and Chronicles.

**The Fivefold Division of the Law**

Something needs to be said at this point about the first division known as 'The Law.' The Books of Moses are known as 'the Pentateuch' from the Greek word *pentateuchos* meaning five-volumed. The Jews knew these books as *the Law*. It took three years of weekly readings in the synagogues to read through the whole. The Law had a foundational place in Israel and retains an honoured place in the Gospel Church. As William Secker explains: 'The *Law* by which God *rules* us, is as dear to Him as the *Gospel* by which He *saves* us.'[14] That Moses has an honourable place in the New Testament church as a faithful servant of God is stated plainly in The Epistle to the Hebrews though that honourable place is not

---

[14] Quoted in I. D. E. Thomas, *op. cit.,* p. 165.

**Books in the Order of the English Bible**
**as found in the Threefold Jewish Canon**

| *The Law* | *The Prophets* | *The Writings* |
|---|---|---|
| The Pentateuch | | |
| | *The Former Prophets* | |
| | Joshua | |
| | Judges | |
| | | Ruth *2.2* |
| | I Samuel | |
| | II Samuel | |
| | I Kings | |
| | II Kings | |
| | | I Chronicles *3.4* |
| | | II Chronicles *3.5* |
| | | Ezra *3.2* |
| | | Nehemiah *3.3* |
| | | Esther *2.5* |
| | | Job *1.3* |
| | | Psalms *1.1* |
| | | Proverbs *1.2* |
| | | Ecclesiastes *2.4* |
| | | Song of Songs *2.1* |
| | *The Latter Prophets* | |
| | Isaiah | |
| | Jeremiah | |
| | | Lamentations *2.3* |
| | Ezekiel | |
| | | Daniel *3.1* |
| | *The Twelve* | |

*Table 3.3*

to be set against Christ. 'Wherefore, holy brethren, partakers of the heavenly calling, consider the Apostle and High Priest of our profession, Christ Jesus; Who was faithful to him that appointed him, as also Moses was faithful in all his house. For this man was counted worthy of more glory than Moses, inasmuch as he who hath builded the house hath more honour than the house. For every house is builded by some man; but he that built all things is God. And Moses verily was faithful in all his house, as a servant, for a testimony of those things which were to be spoken after.'[15]

## The Fivefold Grouping of the New Testament Books

The Westminster Confession provides the following fivefold grouping for the books of the New Testament.

| | |
|---|---|
| *The Gospels* | according to Matthew; Mark; Luke; John |
| *The Acts of the Apostles* | |
| *Paul's Epistles* | Romans; I Corinthians; II Corinthians; Galatians; Ephesians; Philippians; Colossians; I Thessalonians; II Thessalonians; I Timothy; II Timothy; Titus; Philemon; Hebrews |
| *The General Epistles* | The Epistle of James; The first and second Epistles of Peter; The first, second, and third Epistles of John; and The Epistle of Jude |
| *The Revelation of John* | |

Of all of the Old and New Testament books listed, the Confession states: 'All which are given by inspiration of God, to be the rule of faith and life.' Thus each one of the books of the Old Testament and of the New Testament is inspired or God-breathed.

---

[15] Hebrews 3.1–5.

## THE FORMATION OF THE CANON

### The Formation of the Canon of the Old Testament

Various theories have been suggested concerning the development of the Canon of the Old Testament and the recognition of the individual books within it. There are also different views as to how the 'development' of the Canon of the Old Testament relates to the order of the books within the Jewish Canon. If we take seriously the inspiration and authority of Scripture this must be our starting point and we will recognise that the inspired Scripture was authoritative and canonical as soon as it was given. This would be true irrespective of the manner and timing of its recognition by the wider community. The formation of the Canon should thus be approached in relation to the periods in which the different books of the Old Testament were written. Consider *Table 3.4* below.

It can be seen from *Table 3.4* that the books of the Old Testament originated within the period 1400 BC to 401 BC although some regard the Book of Job as dating from an earlier period. The general picture for the completion of the writing of the Old Testament Books is as follows.

### The Pentateuch

The Pentateuch dates from the beginning of this period with Joshua and Judges following.

### The Poetical Literature

The poetical literature is generally dated from the period of the Monarchy around 1000 BC. The books of Samuel would be completed shortly afterwards.

### The Latter Prophets

The Latter Prophets date from 850 BC. with Jeremiah, Daniel and Ezekiel around the time of the exile in the Seventh Century BC.

*Post-exilic Literature*

The Post-exilic literature from the middle of the Sixth Century BC. includes: Haggai, Zechariah, Chronicles, Ezra, Esther, Nehemiah and Malachi.

**The Period of the Formation of the Old Testament Canon**

| Timescale | Years | |
|---|---|---|
| 4000 – 3401 BC | 600 | |
| 3400 – 2401 BC | 1000 | |
| 2400 – 1401 BC | 1000 | |
| 1400 – 401 BC | 1000 | Old Testament Books were completed during this period.[16] |
| 400 BC – AD 600 | 1000 | |
| AD 601 – 1600 | 1000 | |
| AD 1601 – 2000 | 400 | |

*Table 3.4*

## The Formation of the New Testament Canon

Although the formation of the Old Testament Canon spanned *one thousand years* that of the New Testament was accomplished in about *sixty years* commencing around AD 36. This reflected the fact that the times of preparation were ended and that grace and truth *had come* by Jesus Christ.[17] The general picture for the completion of the New Testament books is as follows.

---

[16] Some would place the book of Job at an earlier date.

[17] John 1.17.

53

### The Synoptic Gospels

The approximate dating of the New Testament books belongs to the study of *New Testament Introduction* and there are various views with respect to the time of completion of a number of the books and also concerning which were the first to be produced. However, the Gospels of Matthew, Mark and Luke and the Epistle of James are considered to be in the first twenty years of the period.

### The Epistles of Paul, Peter and Jude and John's Gospel

Towards the end of this twenty-year period the Apostle Paul would have commenced writing his epistles and would continue writing during a period of about another twenty years. The letters of Peter and Jude and the Gospel of John would also be completed towards the close of this second twenty-year period.

### The Epistles of John and the Book of Revelation

The Epistles of John and the Book of Revelation were thought to have been completed towards the end of the first century.

## CONCLUSION

Our overview in this chapter serves as a library brochure for the most precious collection of books in the world to stir us up to get into this Divinely inspired library to read what is there. The scripture assures us that this is the way of true blessing. 'And many other signs truly did Jesus in the presence of his disciples, which are not written in this book: But these are written, that ye might believe that Jesus is the Christ, the Son of God; and that believing ye might have life through his name.'[18]

There are different approaches to schemes for reading through the Bible but usually both the Old Testament and the New Testament should be

---

[18] John 20:30–31.

read each week if not each day. It is convenient to read the Old Testament on a morning and the New Testament on an evening or vice versa. In this way both are read daily. It is important to try to read several chapters each day as in this way it is not too long before the whole of the Scripture is read. This furnishes the reader with a greater opportunity to gain a strategic grasp of the Bible and also to compare scripture with scripture. Some people like to read through the Testaments consecutively and others prefer to have a pre-arranged reading scheme that selects books in a different order.

The attitude of the reader is fundamental. The scriptures should be approached as a unique collection of books, being the very Word of God. To them we must come seeking Christ who is the living bread that came down from heaven to nourish our souls through faith. We must come to the Bible as miners seeking treasure, ready to dig deep to find the pure gold. The reader must come with a conscious sense of searching and with a deep humility of soul as one who cannot understand without the enlightenment of the Holy Spirit. The study of the scriptures must therefore be undertaken prayerfully, that God would be pleased to grant the necessary illumination to bring the light of spiritual understanding to the reader.

It is a good practice to make some notes as one goes along. It helps to fix important lessons upon our mind. It is also a good practice to note down the important teachings of a particular passage. Some recommend the answering of relevant questions such as:

1.  What does this passage teach me about God?

2.  What does the passage teach me about myself?

3.  What does the passage teach me about Christ?

4.  What does the passage tell me about the way of salvation?

5.  What does the passage teach me about the work of the Holy Spirit?

6.  Does the passage have anything to say about the Church and the communion of saints?

7. Does the passage tell me anything about the last things such as the end of time, the resurrection and the final judgement, Heaven and Hell?

As a reader of the Bible you should ask God to give to you a love of his Word that will keep you diligent in searching the scriptures, to confirm in your own heart the things that are most surely believed among us.[19]

---

[19] Luke 1.1.

# Chapter 4

## *The Inspiration Of Scripture*

### *Inspiration – The Apocrypha*

In the previous chapter we saw that the definition of Scripture required consideration: (a) *Extensively* – The Canon, (b) *Intensively* – Inspiration and (c) *Exclusively* – The Apocrypha. We have dealt with the Canon and specified the sixty-six books contained in it and now turn our attention to the specific quality of these books and the reason why the application of the criterion of inspiration excludes the Apocryphal writings.

### INSPIRATION

### *2 Timothy 3.16*

'All scripture is given by inspiration of God, and is profitable for doctrine, for reproof, for correction, for instruction in righteousness...'

### The Meaning of 'Inspiration'

Of the sixty-six books of the Old and New Testaments constituting 'the Holy Scripture' or 'the Word of God written' the Westminster Confession states: 'All which are given by inspiration of God, to be the rule of faith and life.'[1]

The word 'inspiration' is derived from the Latin language. It was used by the Latin translation known as the Vulgate to translate the Greek word *theopneustos* in 2 Timothy 3.16. This Greek word has two elements to it: 'God' (*theo*) and 'breathed' (*pneustos*). These two elements should be the basis of our understanding of *given by inspiration of God* or 'God-inspired'. The emphasis in the original Greek does not fall upon

---

[1] 'The Confession of Faith of the Westminster Assembly of Divines' Chapter 1.2 in S. W. Carruthers (ed.), *The Westminster Confession of Faith* (Manchester: R. Aikman & Son, 1937) p.90.

something 'breathed *in*' by God but the fact that the scriptures are 'breathed *out*' by him. The word *theopneustos* is passive in form so the best concise translation that we could give of it would be 'God-breathed', thus 'all scripture is God-breathed'. From the earliest times of the Jewish Church it was recognized that God's authoritative word of revelation proceeded from his mouth, an evident anthropomorphism. The Scripture did not originate in consequence of human investigation whereby men of God, searching into spiritual things, arrived at insights that they then communicated. They searched into the *meaning* of the revelations that they received but the Word that they received originated with God in such a way that he was the real author of Scripture: 'For the prophecy came not in old time by the will of man: but holy men of God spake as they were moved by the Holy Ghost.'[2] The initiative was not with them and the prophecy was not according to their will, rather the Holy Spirit moved them. God's Spirit was the initiator and the one in control of the situation of the giving of God's Word.

This helps us to understand the balance between Divine authorship and human instrumentality. We must not deny that God used men as men. Their conscious involvement in what they were doing was not suspended; they were active in speaking or writing but at the time they were also passive in being carried along by the Holy Spirit. He was so in control of the situation and of them that they wrote exactly what he intended. Professor E. J. Young comments as follows: 'In being borne by the Spirit the writers were passive; in speaking and writing they were active. This might seem to be a contradiction, but it is not. It is simply an expression of the mystery involved in the truth that the words of Scripture are divine words and yet are also the words of human writers.'[3] We must not seek to probe into the miracle involved. The scriptures do not describe the process. Reformed authors usually describe it as 'organic inspiration' and not 'mechanical inspiration' to guard against the idea that the Holy Spirit used men in an instrumental way; such as we would use a typewriter. We must not reduce the human instruments that God used to the level of unthinking keyboards or elevate them to the

---

[2] 2 Peter 1.21.

[3] Edward J. Young, *Thy Word is Truth: Some Thoughts on the Biblical Doctrine of Inspiration* (Edinburgh: The Banner of Truth Trust, 1963) footnote p.25.

position of original authors of the words written. We must keep the scriptural balance between these two errors and recognise that God used these men as thinking men and yet so superintended the writing of the Scripture that each and every word originated with him as the Divine author. In an article entitled 'Inspiration' in *The Presbyterian Review*, A. A. Hodge and B. B. Warfield provided a thoughtful explanation of this balance in the following words: 'Paul and John and Peter largely drew upon the resources, and followed the lines of their own personal religious experience in the intuitional or the logical development of their doctrine, and their experience had, of course, been previously divinely determined for that very purpose. And in determining their religious experience, God so far forth determined their contributions to Scripture. And He furnished each of the Sacred writers, in addition to that which came to him through natural channels, all the knowledge needed for his appointed task, either by vision, suggestion, dictation or elevation of faculty, or otherwise, according to His will. The natural knowledge came from all sources, as traditions, documents, testimonies, personal observations and recollections; by means also of intuitions, logical process of thought, feeling, experience, etc., and yet all were alike under the general direction of God's providence. The supernatural knowledge became confluent with the natural in a manner which violated no law of reason or of freedom. And throughout the whole of His work the Holy Spirit was present, causing His energies to flow into the spontaneous exercises of the writer's faculties, elevating and directing where need be, and everywhere securing the errorless expression in language of the thought designed by God.'[4]

## The Extent of Inspiration

### Plenary Inspiration

The word *plenary* means 'full'. Thus the term *plenary inspiration* is used to affirm that it is not just the doctrine that is God-breathed but that the full content of the Scripture is inspired. The entire Scripture is God-breathed. We are not left to find the parts of the Bible that are inspired and ignore the rest. All of the Scripture is inspired. This applies to the

---

[4] *Ibid.*, p.97.

specific statements not just to general themes. It applies to matters of scientific or historical fact as well as ethical and doctrinal matters. It descends to the very words.

*Verbal Inspiration*

The apostle Paul is emphatic that the inspiration of the scriptures is verbal inspiration. He did not merely communicate inspired thoughts or doctrines but was given God-breathed words for the purpose of communicating the Christian Faith. Writing of the truths made known by God he states: 'Which things also we speak, not *in the words* which man's wisdom teacheth, but *which the Holy Ghost teacheth*; comparing spiritual things with spiritual.'[5]

## The Significance of Inspiration

The properties of scripture stem from this Divine authorship. If the Scriptures are the Word of God written then it necessarily follows that they are of Divine authority. It must also follow that they are utterly reliable because God is true and they must consequently be true. The Lord Jesus Christ regarded them as unbreakable down to a word. They are thus infallible, free from error, trustworthy and self-authenticating. Concerning the properties of Scripture we may state that the Scriptures are: Holy, Pure, True, Infallible, Inerrant, Trustworthy, Excellent, and Self-authenticating. They are also Sufficient, Perspicuous, Self-interpreting and Authoritative.

*Infallibility*

With respect to infallibility E. J. Young states: 'By the term infallible as applied to the Bible, we mean simply that the Scripture possesses an indefectible authority. As our Lord Himself said 'it cannot be broken' [John 10:31]. It can never fail in its judgements and statements. All that it teaches is of unimpeachable, absolute authority, and cannot be contravened, contradicted, or gainsaid. Scripture is unfailing, incapable of proving false, erroneous, or mistaken. Though heaven and earth

---

[5] 1 Corinthians 2.13.

should pass away, its words of truth will stand forever. It cannot be changed nor destroyed.'[6]

*Inerrancy*

Concerning the word *inerrant* E. J. Young says: 'By this word we mean that the Scriptures possess the quality of freedom from error. They are exempt from the liability of mistake, incapable of error. In all their teachings they are in perfect accord with the truth.'[7] Wherever we access the *Scripture* we find this utter reliability. It is often thought that we cannot speak in terms of possessing the *inerrant* Scripture now because of variants between manuscripts but it is obvious that if a reading is incorrect that reading is *not* Scripture but *a departure from* Scripture and cannot, therefore, affect the inerrancy of *Scripture*. What is necessary is to eliminate erroneous readings by reference to the body of reliable extant manuscripts. However, inerrancy is about more than the individual words and applies to the total content. It is not just that the scriptures are without error in the doctrines and morality taught, they are without error in respect of all that they contain.

This is not to say that there are not *apparent* errors and *apparent* contradictions in the scriptures. At first sight it may seem that there *are* errors and after much study it may not be possible to reconcile all of the data; but this is just to say that more study is necessary or new insights into the problem are needed, or that, on the basis of the available information, a solution cannot be found. This has been the case with various passages and then new archaeological discoveries have brought more information to light that have helped to understand the meaning. Nor must we be disturbed by the allegations that science has proved the Bible wrong. When we investigate properly, what we find is that human *theories* of origins are in conflict with the Bible and that it can be shown that the Scripture is not in conflict with the scientific *facts*.

Nor must we assume that every time that a parallel passage or quotation is not verbatim that this is to be attributed to error. In connection with quotations it is necessary to take into consideration the source of the

---

[6] E. J. Young, *op. cit.*, p.113.
[7] *Ibid.*

quotation, which may be the original Hebrew, or the Septuagint Greek translation of it. Also the purpose of the quotation is relevant and the fact that the inspired author may want to bring out the full meaning more clearly by an appropriate but accurate translation. With respect to parallel passages it must be kept in mind that different accounts can give a true report without using identical words, as takes place daily in the evidence of witnesses in our law courts. Writers may have different perspectives and select what is appropriate for their purpose without distorting the truth. This is also relevant in relation to the different order of events that we encounter in the opening chapters of Genesis and in the Gospels. We have to remember that one passage might be in *chronological order* whereas another is arranged *topically*. When this is taken into consideration we can see that the alleged contradiction is attributable to the *interpreter* not the *author*. This is particularly the case where those who hold to the *inerrancy* of Scripture are regarded as obliged to a *literal interpretation* of Scripture. But it is obvious that one can hold to inerrancy and at the same time accept that the Bible contains poetry and parable as well as historical prose or prophecy and symbol as well as doctrinal statements. Interpretation must take into consideration grammatical, historical and stylistic considerations and we are not prevented from mature interpretation just because we hold to inerrancy. Indeed a high view of the inerrancy of Scripture demands that we engage in the most careful exegesis.

## THE APOCRYPHA

The Confession's statement with respect to the Apocrypha is that: 'The books commonly called Apocrypha, not being of divine inspiration, are no part of the canon of the Scripture; and therefore are of no authority in the Church of God, nor to be any otherwise approved, or made use of, than other human writings.' A. A. Hodge comments as follows on this passage: 'The word Apocrypha (anything hidden) has been applied to certain ancient writings whose authorship is not manifest, and for which unfounded claims have been set up for a place in the canon. Some of these have been associated with the Old and some with the New Testament. In this section of the Confession, however, the name is applied principally to those spurious scriptures for which a place is claimed in the Old Testament canon by the Roman Church. These are

*Tobit*, *Wisdom*, *Judith*, *Ecclesiasticus*, *Baruch*, and the two books of *Maccabees*. They also prefix to the book of Daniel the *History of Susannah*; and insert in the third chapter the *Song of the Three Children*; and add to the end of the book the *History of Bel and the Dragon*.

> 'That these books have no right to a place in the canon is proved by the following facts: (1) They never formed a part of the Hebrew Scriptures. They have always been rejected by the Jews, to whose guardianship the Old Testament Scriptures were committed. (2) None of them were ever quoted by Christ or the apostles. (3) They were never embraced in the list of the canonical books by the early Fathers; and even in the Roman Church their authority was not accepted by the most learned and candid men until after it was made an article of faith by the Council of Trent, late in the sixteenth century. (4) The internal evidence presented by their contents disproves their claims. None of them make any claim to inspiration, while the best of them disclaim it. Some of them consist of childish fables, and inculcate bad morals.'[8]

It should be noted that the Confession wisely indicates that the reason for a book's inclusion in the canon of Scripture is its 'divine inspiration' and the reason for a book's exclusion from the canon of Scripture is the absence of 'divine inspiration.' As William Hendriksen explains: 'What should be emphasized, however, is that not because the church, upon a certain date, long ago, made an official decision... do these books constitute the inspired Bible; on the contrary, the sixty-six books, by their very contents, immediately attest themselves to the hearts of all Spirit-indwelt men as being the living oracles of God. Hence, believers are filled with deep reverence whenever they hear the voice of God addressing them from Holy Writ... All scripture is canonical because God made it so!'[9]

---

[8] A. A. Hodge, *The Confession of Faith: A Handbook of Christian Doctrine Expounding The Westminster Confession* (Edinburgh: The Banner of Truth Trust, 1964) p.33.

[9] William Hendriksen, *A Commentary on I & II Timothy and Titus* (Edinburgh: The Banner of Truth Trust, 1964) p.302.

# Chapter 5

## *The Authority Of Scripture*

*Scripture Authority – Persuasion of the Authority of Scripture*

### SCRIPTURE AUTHORITY

*2 Timothy 3.1–17*

'This know also, that in the last days perilous times shall come. For men shall be lovers of their own selves, covetous, boasters, proud, blasphemers, disobedient to parents, unthankful, unholy, Without natural affection, trucebreakers, false accusers, incontinent, fierce, despisers of those that are good, Traitors, heady, highminded, lovers of pleasures more than lovers of God; Having a form of godliness, but denying the power thereof: from such turn away. For of this sort are they which creep into houses, and lead captive silly women laden with sins, led away with divers lusts, Ever learning, and never able to come to the knowledge of the truth. Now as Jannes and Jambres withstood Moses, so do these also resist the truth: men of corrupt minds, reprobate concerning the faith. But they shall proceed no further: for their folly shall be manifest unto all men, as theirs also was. But thou hast fully known my doctrine, manner of life, purpose, faith, longsuffering, charity, patience, Persecutions, afflictions, which came unto me at Antioch, at Iconium, at Lystra; what persecutions I endured: but out of them all the Lord delivered me. Yea, and all that will live godly in Christ Jesus shall suffer persecution. But evil men and seducers shall wax worse and worse, deceiving, and being deceived. But continue thou in the things which thou hast learned and hast been assured of, knowing of whom thou hast learned them; And that from a child thou hast known the holy scriptures, which are able to make thee wise unto salvation through faith which is in Christ Jesus. All scripture is given by inspiration of God, and is profitable for doctrine, for reproof, for correction, for instruction in righteousness: That the man of God may be perfect, throughly furnished unto all good works.'

The words of John 3.16 are often quoted as an encapsulation of salvation: 'For God so loved the world, that he gave his only begotten Son, that whosoever believeth in him should not perish, but have everlasting life.' In these words we have the *origin* of salvation in the love of God, the *foundation* of it in the atoning death of the incarnate Son, the *way* of salvation through faith in him and the two-sided *benefit* of not perishing and of having eternal life. 2 Timothy 3.16 is in one sense *more* fundamental. It affirms the *origin, authority* and *usefulness* of the Bible as the Word of God. If the scriptures of the Old and New Testaments are not *reliable* then what trust could we place in the words of John 3.16? We must thus be persuaded of the authority of Scripture. In these words of Paul we see that the scriptures are (1) a *revelation* from God, (2) the *rule* of faith and life and (3) to be *received* as the Word of God.

**The Scriptures are a *Revelation* from God**

Paul had just spoken of Timothy's upbringing from his infancy: 'from a child thou hast known the holy scriptures, which are able to make thee wise unto salvation through faith which is in Christ Jesus.'[1] The original Greek emphasizes the fact that it was from when he was a baby. Luke uses the same word *brephos* to describe an infant in the womb.[2] A faithful grandmother and a faithful mother had taught Timothy the Old Testament sacred writings from his earliest years. Thus Timothy must not allow his faith to be shaken by such things as: the evil of the times (verse 1), apostate formalism (verse 5), false teaching (verse 6), persecutions (verses 11–12), declining spirituality or increasing wickedness (verse 13). We are to be comforted by the fact that the Scriptures we rely upon are a revelation from God. In this they are

[1] 2 Timothy 3.15.
[2] Luke 1.41.

unique. They stand above all other writings and teachings as 'inspired' by God. 'Given by inspiration of God' is in the original Greek but one word, *theopneustos*. It combines the word for *God* with that for *spirit* or *breath*. Thus it literally means *God-inspired* or *God-breathed*. Simply put, the Bible is a product of God's Spirit. As William Hendriksen explains: ' "all scripture" owes its origin and contents to the divine breath, the Spirit of God.'[3]

There are two important considerations to remember in this connection. (1) This inspiration is *organic* and not *mechanical*. The Holy Spirit used the human authors of the scriptures as human beings not typewriters. Their personalities and talents were not suspended but utilized. (2) Inspiration applies to *all* Scripture not just *some* Scripture. The Apostle Paul described the Old Testament as 'the oracles of God'[4] and the Lord Jesus Christ referred to its different parts saying that 'all things must be fulfilled, which were written in the law of Moses, and in the prophets, and in the psalms, concerning me.'[5] The Apostle Peter attributes the same nature to the New Testament letters of the Apostle Paul: 'As also in all his epistles, speaking in them of these things; in which are some things hard to be understood, which they that are unlearned and unstable wrest, as they do also *the other scriptures*, unto their own destruction.'[6] Thus *all* that is scripture is inspired. As Thomas Watson states: 'The two Testaments are the two lips by which God hath spoken to us.'[7]

## The Scriptures are the *Rule* of Faith and Life

It must follow that if God has given the Scripture that his authority is in it. John Whitlock explained the practical implication of this as follows: 'When you hear the Word, say, "There God spoke to my soul." Men forget truths because they are apt to put them off to others, and not to

---

[3] William Hendriksen, *A Commentary on I & II Timothy and Titus* (Edinburgh: The Banner of Truth Trust, 1964) p. 302.

[4] Romans 3.2.

[5] Luke 24.44.

[6] 2 Peter 3.16

[7] Quoted in I. D. E. Thomas, *The Golden Treasury of Puritan Quotations* (Edinburgh: The Banner of Truth Trust, 1997) p. 34.

look on themselves as concerned in them.'[8] If one that you love speaks to you, you do not turn a deaf ear. As Scripture is inspired and authoritative it is *profitable* for the uses God designed it for. Paul gives four *uses* of the Scripture: 'for doctrine, for reproof, for correction, for instruction in righteousness.' (1) *Doctrine* or *teaching*. The scriptures are designed to teach us saving truth. There is no higher imparting of knowledge than that which issues in eternal life. When Christ is believed upon salvation results. (2) *Reproof.* This involves exposing, refuting and reproving what is erroneous. (3) *Correction.* To correct is to put onto the right path, as when the traveller who does not know the way is given clear directions without which he would still be lost and astray. (4) *Instruction* or *training*. The training in view is instruction in righteousness. By imparting true knowledge, error is exposed and the right path disclosed and all is consummated in the outcome of practical godliness. The surgeon who has all of the knowledge but who never undertakes any operations has knowledge but it has no practical outcome. The importance of practical living is emphasized in the Book of Proverbs, which is concerned with practical not speculative wisdom. God's purpose in giving the scriptures is 'that the man of God may be perfect, throughly furnished unto all good works' (verse 17). The 'fully-fitted' kitchen is the one in which every imaginable piece of equipment is included. Such is the idea of 'throughly furnished', nothing is to be lacking, everything necessary is to be present and the scriptures are given to ensure this.

## The Scriptures are to be *Received* as the Word of God

Having seen some of the excellences of the scriptures we might be caused to ask: Why does the Bible not make the changes in my life that it should? What is the problem? The trouble with too many is that their reliance is placed upon the church, upon the preacher or upon some other that they admire. Obedience becomes a matter of *human* authority and tradition and consequently seems less important. The Westminster Confession puts matters otherwise: 'The authority of the Holy Scripture, for which it ought to be believed and obeyed, dependeth not upon the

---

[8] Quoted *ibid.*, p. 36.

testimony of any man, or Church; but wholly upon God (who is truth itself) the author thereof: and therefore it is to be received because it is the Word of God.'[9] The Apostle Paul rejoiced to see faith and obedience that was rooted in recognition of the authority of God. 'For this cause also thank we God without ceasing, because, when ye received the word of God which ye heard of us, ye received it not as the word of men, but as it is in truth, the word of God, which effectually worketh also in you that believe.'[10]

There is a practical lesson for us here. We are glad that every word of the Scripture is reliable but how much response do we give to it? If we consider again its purpose we see that the divine intention is that the study of the scriptures should produce godliness; by which is meant a full-orbed Christian life conformed to the image of Christ and pleasing to God.

## PERSUASION OF THE AUTHORITY OF SCRIPTURE

### *Luke 4.16–30*

'And he came to Nazareth, where he had been brought up: and, as his custom was, he went into the synagogue on the sabbath day, and stood up for to read. And there was delivered unto him the book of the prophet Esaias. And when he had opened the book, he found the place where it was written, The Spirit of the Lord is upon me, because he hath anointed me to preach the gospel to the poor; he hath sent me to heal the brokenhearted, to preach deliverance to the captives, and recovering of sight to the blind, to set at liberty them that are bruised, To preach the acceptable year of the Lord. And he closed the book, and he gave it again to the minister, and sat down. And the eyes of all them that were in the synagogue were fastened on him. And he began to say unto them, This day is this scripture fulfilled in your

---

[9] 'The Confession of Faith of the Westminster Assembly of Divines' Chapter 1.4 in S. W. Carruthers (ed.), *The Westminster Confession of Faith* (Manchester: R. Aikman & Son, 1937) p.91.

[10] 1 Thessalonians 2.13.

ears. And all bare him witness, and wondered at the gracious words which proceeded out of his mouth. And they said, Is not this Joseph's son? And he said unto them, Ye will surely say unto me this proverb, Physician, heal thyself: whatsoever we have heard done in Capernaum, do also here in thy country. And he said, Verily I say unto you, No prophet is accepted in his own country. But I tell you of a truth, many widows were in Israel in the days of Elias, when the heaven was shut up three years and six months, when great famine was throughout all the land; But unto none of them was Elias sent, save unto Sarepta, a city of Sidon, unto a woman that was a widow. And many lepers were in Israel in the time of Eliseus the prophet; and none of them was cleansed, saving Naaman the Syrian. And all they in the synagogue, when they heard these things, were filled with wrath, And rose up, and thrust him out of the city, and led him unto the brow of the hill whereon their city was built, that they might cast him down headlong. But he passing through the midst of them went his way…'

For over two hundred years the authority of the Bible has been under particular attack. New discoveries were supposed to have proved it to be in error at so many points. However, continued research has shown that many of the criticisms are themselves erroneous. The patriarchs, for example, were regarded as merely legendary figures and the accounts concerning them as late inventions; but archaeology has shown exact correspondences between the accounts and modern discoveries as to the way of life in the second millennium BC. But much damage has been done to people's confidence in the Bible. However, we should note that what has been damaged is people's subjective inward confidence not the objective outward fact of the authority of the scriptures. The saying of C. H. Spurgeon is to the point: 'Defend the Bible! I'd rather defend a lion!' The problem is not with what the Bible is but with what people think that it is. This accounts for Paul's thankfulness with respect to the Thessalonian Christians. In relation to Luke 4.16–30 we should consider (1) *Esteem* for the Scripture, (2) *Evidences* of its authority and (3) The *effectual application* of it to the heart.

## *Esteem* for the Scripture

The Westminster Confession in Chapter 1, Paragraph 5 states: 'We may be moved and induced by the testimony of the Church to a high and reverent esteem of the Holy Scripture.'[11] John Flavel comments on the excellency and sufficiency of the scriptures as follows: 'The Scriptures teach us the best way of living, the noblest way of suffering, and the most comfortable way of dying.'[12] In the Jewish synagogues of our Saviour's day there was one collection of books, thirty-nine in all. We know them as the Old Testament. These were what were read. 'And he came to Nazareth, where he had been brought up: and, as his custom was, he went into the synagogue on the sabbath day, and stood up for to read. And there was delivered unto him the book of the prophet Esaias.'[13] The Jewish church of that day handed to Jesus, the eternal Son of God incarnate, part of the Scripture or written Word they commended. These were the books that they recognized as the revealed Word of God. What would Jesus have thought had they handed to him Plato's Republic or Homer's poetry? The answer is plain to be seen from the Saviour's actions on another occasion: 'And said unto them that sold doves, Take these things hence; make not my Father's house an house of merchandise. And his disciples remembered that it was written, The zeal of thine house hath eaten me up.'[14] As to non-canonical books, the Saviour would not have used them in God's House. But with respect to the portion of the Old Testament we read: 'And when he had opened the book, he found the place where it was written...'[15]

By his example here and on other occasions, and by his instructions, the Lord Jesus Christ would have us to esteem the scriptures and only them. So we have that example of his instruction when he said to the two disciples on the Emmaus Road: 'O fools, and slow of heart to believe all that the prophets have spoken: Ought not Christ to have suffered these

---

[11] 'The Confession of Faith of the Westminster Assembly of Divines' Chapter 1.5 in S. W. Carruthers (ed.), *The Westminster Confession of Faith* (Manchester: R. Aikman & Son, 1937) p.91.

[12] Quoted in I. D. E. Thomas, *op. cit.,* p. 33.

[13] Luke 4.16–17a.

[14] John 2.16–17.

[15] Luke 4.17b.

things, and to enter into his glory? And beginning at Moses and all the prophets, he expounded unto them in all the scriptures the things concerning himself.'[16] The true church must have no other testimony. We have one answer to the question, How can a man be wise unto salvation? It is the answer that is required by the instruction of the Apostle Paul to Timothy: 'But continue thou in the things which thou hast learned and hast been assured of, knowing of whom thou hast learned them; And that from a child thou hast known *the holy scriptures, which are able to make thee wise unto salvation* through faith which is in Christ Jesus. *All scripture* is given by inspiration of God, and is profitable for doctrine, for reproof, for correction, for instruction in righteousness: That the man of God may be perfect, throughly furnished unto all good works.'[17] So Ezekiel Hopkins states: 'The Bible is the statute-book of God's Kingdom, wherein is comprised the whole body of the heavenly law, the perfect rules of a holy life, and the sure promises of a glorious one.'[18]

## *Evidences* of the Authority of Scripture

The Westminster Confession identifies evidences of the authority of Scripture as follows: 'the heavenliness of the matter, the efficacy of the doctrine, the majesty of the style, the consent of all the parts, the scope of the whole (which is, to give all glory to God) the full discovery it makes of the only way of man's salvation, the many other incomparable excellencies, and the entire perfection thereof, are arguments whereby it doth abundantly evidence itself to be the Word of God...'[19] They are all seen in this one brief extract: 'The Spirit of the Lord is upon me, because he hath anointed me to preach the gospel to the poor; he hath sent me to heal the brokenhearted, to preach deliverance to the captives, and recovering of sight to the blind, to set at liberty them that are bruised, To preach the acceptable year of the Lord.'[20] Note the following. (1) *The*

---

[16] Luke 24.25–27.

[17] 2 Timothy 3.14–17.

[18] Quoted in I. D. E. Thomas, *op. cit.,* p. 32.

[19] 'The Confession of Faith of the Westminster Assembly of Divines' Chapter 1.5 in S. W. Carruthers (ed.), *The Westminster Confession of Faith* (Manchester: R. Aikman & Son, 1937) p. 91.

[20] Luke 4.18–19

*heavenliness of the matter.* The reading from the prophet begins with the Triune God: the Spirit, the Lord God and the eternal Son. (2) *The efficacy of the doctrine.* What power there is in the message of the Gospel preached to the poor! Those who are saved know the effect of God's Word in accordance with the Saviour's assurance: 'Then said Jesus to those Jews which believed on him, If ye continue in my word, then are ye my disciples indeed; And ye shall know the truth, and the truth shall make you free.'[21] The pragmatist says, it works, so it's right for me. He must see it work *before* he believes. But Christ says, believe, and then you will know that it works. (3) *The majesty of the style.* How evident this is in the prophecy of Isaiah. Not only in the passage that the Saviour read but again and again. Consider the following. 'Comfort ye, comfort ye my people, saith your God. Speak ye comfortably to Jerusalem, and cry unto her, that her warfare is accomplished, that her iniquity is pardoned: for she hath received of the Lord's hand double for all her sins...'[22] 'Behold, the Lord God will come with strong hand, and his arm shall rule for him: behold, his reward is with him, and his work before him. He shall feed his flock like a shepherd: he shall gather the lambs with his arm, and carry them in his bosom, and shall gently lead those that are with young.'[23] (4) *The consent of all the parts.* The prophecy comes from Isaiah 61 but there is perfect correspondence with Luke centuries later. 'And he began to say unto them, This day is this scripture fulfilled in your ears.'[24] (5) *The scope of the whole.* Scripture is like a spider's web. There are so many strands making one intricate whole of beauty and utility which, when the dew of the Spirit is upon it, astounds us with its grandeur. (6) *The full discovery it makes of the only way of man's salvation.* Is this not our greatest delight with it? The Scripture really has the answer to the needs of sinners. Within the scriptures we find the Messiah, the prophet and the preacher, the healer, the deliverer, the enlightener, the one who sets us free. Of *himself* Jesus says: 'The Spirit of the Lord is upon me, because he hath *anointed* me to *preach* the gospel to the poor; he hath sent me to *heal* the brokenhearted,

---

[21] John 8.31–32.

[22] Isaiah 40.1–2.

[23] Isaiah 40.10–15.

[24] Luke 4.21.

to preach *deliverance* to the captives, and recovering of *sight* to the blind, to set at *liberty* them that are bruised, To preach the acceptable year of the Lord.'[25] For in the atonement of Christ there is reconciliation and forgiveness to all who believe that being justified by faith alone they might have life eternal. (7) *The many other incomparable excellencies, and the entire perfection thereof.* Who could presume to put the words of men into the hand of Christ? What he was given and what he received was the most excellent and perfect Word of God.

## The *Effectual* Application of the Word to the Heart

The Jews had the Word of God written.[26] The Jews in the synagogue at Nazareth had the word of Christ vocal.[27] They had the testimony of their own consciences: 'And all bare him witness, and wondered at the gracious words which proceeded out of his mouth. And they said, Is not this Joseph's son?'[28] But they did not believe! 'He said unto them, Ye will surely say unto me this proverb, Physician, heal thyself: whatsoever we have heard done in Capernaum, do also here in thy country. And he said, Verily I say unto you, No prophet is accepted in his own country... And all they in the synagogue, when they heard these things, were filled with wrath.'[29] How circumspect we need to be concerning the human heart, which is 'deceitful above all things and desperately wicked.'[30] What a reaction we have here to the truth! They 'rose up, and thrust him out of the city, and led him unto the brow of the hill whereon their city was built, that they might cast him down headlong.'[31]

How clear it is that nothing will secure saving faith but the application of God's Word to our hearts by his own Holy Spirit. The Messiah says, 'The Spirit of the Lord is upon me.' It had to be so 'To appoint unto them that mourn in Zion, to give unto them beauty for ashes, the oil of

---

[25] Luke 4.18–19.

[26] Luke 4.17–19.

[27] Luke 4.20–21.

[28] Luke 4.22.

[29] Luke 4.23–24, 28.

[30] Jeremiah 17.9.

[31] Luke 4.29.

joy for mourning, the garment of praise for the spirit of heaviness; that they might be called trees of righteousness, the planting of the Lord, that he might be glorified.'[32] Weeds plant *themselves* but the husbandman diligently prepares good soil for the precious seed. Thus the Confession states with respect to the authority of the Scripture: 'Our full persuasion and assurance of the infallible truth and divine authority thereof, is from the inward work of the Holy Spirit bearing witness by and with the Word in our hearts.'[33]

The Bible has been given to the church for *assured* faith. This Luke affirms: 'Forasmuch as many have taken in hand to set forth in order a declaration of *those things which are most surely believed among us,* Even as they delivered them unto us, which from the beginning were eyewitnesses, and ministers of the word; It seemed good to me also, having had perfect understanding of all things from the very first, to write unto thee in order, most excellent Theophilus, *That thou mightest know the certainty of those things, wherein thou hast been instructed.'*[34] Thus Thomas Watson advises: 'Leave not off reading the Bible till you find your heart warmed... Let it not only inform you, but inflame you.'[35]

---

[32] Isaiah 61.3.

[33] 'The Confession of Faith of the Westminster Assembly of Divines' Chapter 1.5c in S. W. Carruthers (ed.), *The Westminster Confession of Faith* (Manchester: R. Aikman & Son, 1937) p. 91.

[34] Luke 1.1–4.

[35] Quoted in I. D. E. Thomas, *op. cit.,* p. 36.

# Chapter 6

## *The Sufficiency Of Scripture*

*2 Timothy 3.14–17*

'But continue thou in the things which thou hast learned and hast been assured of, knowing of whom thou hast learned them; And that from a child thou hast known the holy scriptures, which are able to make thee wise unto salvation through faith which is in Christ Jesus. All scripture is given by inspiration of God, and is profitable for doctrine, for reproof, for correction, for instruction in righteousness: That the man of God may be perfect, throughly furnished unto all good works.'

Many folk still have Bibles in their homes. School children and students will consult them when they have assignments to do or examinations to pass. But they remain ignorant of the spiritual message of the scriptures. They have no personal experience of the fruits of Christ's atoning work such as repentance, saving faith, justification and sanctification. This is not new. The Apostle Paul had to warn Timothy of the *'form* of godliness'* where the *power* of the Gospel is unknown. It is thus imperative to make proper use of the Holy Scriptures: (1) as a *sufficient revelation* of the way of salvation; (2) seeking a *spiritual understanding* of them; and (3) *sensibly ordering* things indifferent in the light of their teachings.

### The *Sufficiency* of Scripture

We must understand that the Bible is a sufficient revelation of the way of salvation. Twice Paul assures Timothy of this: 'from a child thou hast known the holy scriptures, *which are able to make thee wise unto salvation* through faith which is in Christ Jesus'; and again: 'All scripture is given by inspiration of God, and is profitable for doctrine, for reproof, for correction, for instruction in righteousness: *That the man of God may be perfect, throughly furnished unto all good works.*' The significance of this is stated by the Westminster Confession as follows: 'The whole counsel of God concerning all things necessary for His own glory, man's salvation, faith, and life, is either expressly set down in Scripture, or by good and necessary consequence may be deduced from Scripture: unto which nothing at any time is to be added, whether by new revelations of the Spirit, or traditions of men.'[1]

We can see from this that the Bible is complete in itself. Perhaps nowhere more than with computers do we experience the frustration of the incompleteness of books? You have the hardware and software manuals, perhaps two inches thick, but when you consult them they do not have the information that you need to know. It is not so with the scriptures, as Paul shows from his charge to the Ephesian elders: 'Wherefore I take you to record this day, that I am pure from the blood of all men. For I have not shunned to declare unto you *all the counsel of God*.'[2] When the preacher has faithfully expounded the scriptures, the hearer has heard the needful truth! 'As if he had said, on this the last day we shall spend together, or the last day of our meeting upon earth, I testify etc. The fact thus solemnly attested is, that if they perished it would not be his fault, or for want of faithful warning and instruction upon his part.'[3] Hence the Apostolic challenge to them: 'Ye know, from the first day that I came into Asia, after what manner I have been with you at all seasons, Serving the Lord with all humility of mind, and with many tears, and temptations, which befell me by the lying in wait of the Jews: And how I kept back nothing that was profitable unto you, but have shewed you, and have taught you publickly, and from house to house, Testifying both to the Jews, and also to the Greeks, repentance toward God, and faith toward our Lord Jesus Christ.'[4] *Repentance toward God*, and *faith toward the Lord Jesus Christ*, such, experimentally, is the sum of it all.

---

[1] 'The Confession of Faith of the Westminster Assembly of Divines' Chapter 1.6 in S. W. Carruthers (ed.), *The Westminster Confession of Faith* (Manchester: R. Aikman & Son, 1937) p.91.

[2] Acts 20.26–27.

[3] J. A. Alexander, *A Commentary on The Acts of the Apostles* (Edinburgh: The Banner of Truth Trust, 1984) p.248.

[4] Acts 20.18b–21.

It is important in this connection to realize that the Bible is to be interpreted *as a whole*. Some want to insist that every matter is expressly stated but it is legitimate to 'deduce' or *draw conclusions from* scriptural statements. Thus the Apostle John states: 'In the beginning was the Word, and the Word was with God, and the Word was God... And the Word was made flesh, and dwelt among us, (and we beheld his glory, the glory as of the only begotten of the Father,) full of grace and truth.'[5] It follows *by necessary consequence*, and without any express statement regarding each one, that Christ, being Divine, is possessed of every attribute of God. So Paul assures the Colossians that 'it pleased the Father that in him should all fulness dwell'[6] and that 'in him dwelleth all the fulness of the Godhead bodily'[7] *and that consequently* Christians 'are complete in him, which is the head of all principality and power.'[8] What *necessarily* follows from one statement is to be believed.

In view of the sufficiency and completeness of Scripture the Bible requires no supplementation and is not to be supplemented whether by alleged revelation or human tradition. So we find at the close of the Bible the words:

> 'For I testify unto every man that heareth the words of the prophecy of this book, If any man shall add unto these things, God shall add unto him the plagues that are written in this book: And if any man shall take away from the words of the book of this prophecy, God shall take away his part out of the book of life, and out of the holy city, and from the things which are written in this book.'[9]

Henry comments: 'This sanction is like a flaming sword, to guard the canon of the scripture from profane hands. Such a fence as this God set about the law (Deut. iv. 2), and the whole Old Testament (Mal. iv. 4), and now in the most solemn manner about the whole Bible, assuring us that it is a book of the most sacred nature, divine authority, and of the

---

[5] John 1.1,14.

[6] Colossians 1.19.

[7] Colossians 2.9.

[8] Colossians 2.10.

[9] Revelation 22.18–19.

last importance, and therefore the peculiar care of the great God.'[10] Nothing could be clearer concerning the inviolability of the written Word of God. It is not to be added to, nor is anything to be taken from it. Faith is to rest *exclusively* upon the Word of God applied by his Spirit: 'And my speech and my preaching was not with enticing words of man's wisdom, but in demonstration of the Spirit and of power: That your faith should not stand in the wisdom of men, but in the power of God.'[11]

### *Spiritual* Understanding of Scripture is to be Sought

The scriptures never suggest that it is enough to outwardly hear the Word of God in order to be saved by it. In fact the Lord Jesus Christ taught that without spiritual enlightenment outward hearing does not help. There must be a *spiritual* hearing.

Consider the Saviour's own words:

> 'Therefore speak I to them in parables: because they seeing see not; and hearing they hear not, neither do they understand. And in them is fulfilled the prophecy of Esaias, which saith, By hearing ye shall hear, and shall not understand; and seeing ye shall see, and shall not perceive: For this people's heart is waxed gross, and their ears are dull of hearing, and their eyes they have closed; lest at any time they should see with their eyes, and hear with their ears, and should understand with their heart, and should be converted, and I should heal them. But blessed are your eyes, for they see: and your ears, for they hear.'[12]

One can know all of the language but still have no spiritual discernment of its significance. Thus the Westminster Divines confessed: 'Nevertheless we acknowledge the inward illumination of the Spirit of

---

[10] Matthew Henry, *An Exposition of the Old and New Testament, Vol. VI. – Acts to Revelation* (London: James Nisbet & Co., Limited, undated)

[11] 1 Corinthians 2.4–5

[12] Matthew 13.13–16.

God to be necessary for the saving understanding of such things as are revealed in the Word...'[13]

Notwithstanding the sufficiency of the Scripture *we* are not sufficient of ourselves to understand it because of our natural depravity and spiritual darkness of mind. So Paul states: 'This I say therefore, and testify in the Lord, that ye henceforth walk not as other Gentiles walk, *in the vanity of their mind*, Having *the understanding darkened*, being alienated from the life of God *through the ignorance that is in them*, because of *the blindness of their heart...*'[14] Coming to the Bible with self-confidence is like coming to the well with a bucket full of holes. We will know nothing of the fountains of living water that are in Christ. Consider the Psalmist's prayer: *'Teach me, O Lord, the way of thy statutes*; and I shall keep it unto the end. *Give me understanding, and I shall keep thy law*; yea, I shall observe it with my whole heart.'[15] See the prayer of Paul: 'Wherefore I also, after I heard of your faith in the Lord Jesus, and love unto all the saints, Cease not to give thanks for you, making mention of you in my prayers; That the God of our Lord Jesus Christ, the Father of glory, may give unto you *the spirit of wisdom and revelation in the knowledge of him: The eyes of your understanding being enlightened*; that ye may know what is the hope of his calling, and what the riches of the glory of his inheritance in the saints...'[16] It was the touch of *Jesus* that gave the blind their sight. The following comment of Swinnock is worth pondering: 'I wonder not that many professors disown the Lord Jesus, when they are ignorant why they at any time owned Him... He that follows Christ, *he knoweth not why*, will forsake Him, *he knoweth not how.*'[17] (Italics mine)

---

[13] 'The Confession of Faith of the Westminster Assembly of Divines' Chapter 1.6 in S. W. Carruthers (ed.), *The Westminster Confession of Faith* (Manchester: R. Aikman & Son, 1937) p. 91.

[14] Ephesians 4.17–18.

[15] Psalm 119.33–34.

[16] Ephesians 1.15–18.

[17] Quoted in I. D. E. Thomas, *The Golden Treasury of Puritan Quotations* (Edinburgh: The Banner of Truth Trust, 1997) p. 235.

## The *Sensible Ordering* of 'Things Indifferent' in the Light of Scripture

Sometimes when we speak about instituted worship people want to evade the force of the regulation of the parts of worship by bringing in all sorts of red herrings about details that are not revealed in Scripture, such as the place of meeting or the ringing of a bell. The Westminster Confession is very circumspect concerning the completeness of the scriptures and a very balanced statement is given. The Divines state that the scriptures contain 'all things necessary' but go on to say: 'Nevertheless we acknowledge the inward illumination of the Spirit of God to be necessary for the saving understanding of such things as are revealed in the Word: and that there are some circumstances concerning the worship of God, and government of the Church, common to human actions and societies, which are to be ordered by the light of nature and Christian prudence, according to the general rules of the Word, which are always to be observed.'[18] The reference here is not to the *parts* or *forms* of worship but to the *circumstances* of worship, that is, the surrounding things.

In the wilderness Israel had a tent.[19] Now there is nothing wrong with tent meetings but it would be contrary to *the general rules of the Word* to make tent meetings obligatory on the basis of Acts 7.44 because we know that the place where believers meet is no longer prescribed. In ordinary circumstances it would be contrary to *Christian prudence* to suggest tent meetings for the winter months in the colder climes of the Northern hemisphere, though it would not be a problem in warmer climates. This would be a matter *common to human actions and societies, which are to be ordered by the light of nature.* The same light of nature would teach the Scottish Covenanters that, if the only place that they could safely worship God were on the windswept moor, then they would need to wrap up in their warmest clothing for those occasions. But with respect to what entered into the celebration of the Lord's Supper on the heather they would *not* look upon the actions required, the breaking of the bread and so on, as *common to human actions and societies... to be ordered by the light of nature and Christian prudence, according to*

---

[18] 'The Confession of Faith of the Westminster Assembly of Divines' Chapter 1.6 in S. W. Carruthers (ed.), *The Westminster Confession of Faith* (Manchester: R. Aikman & Son, 1937) p.91.

[19] Acts 7.44.

*the general rules of the Word…* but rather as *specifically* regulated by the Word of God.

Often people confuse such scripturalness of practice with legalism. It is an easy excuse. For them attention to detail is equivalent to legalism and indicative of a legalistic spirit. If such were so then Jesus would be a legalist. No one ever gave more attention to detail in the things that pleased God than the Saviour did. The 'Great Commission' is phrased in terms of comprehensiveness: 'Go ye therefore, and teach all nations, baptizing them in the name of the Father, and of the Son, and of the Holy Ghost: Teaching them to observe *all things whatsoever I have commanded you*: and, lo, I am with you alway, even unto the end of the world. Amen.'[20] Legalism by way of contrast attributes merit to human actions, it elevates human tradition above the Word of God and makes prescriptive what God does not. Legalism is the opposite of the disposition of soul of the true believer who *wants* to do things *God's way* because we love him who first loved us. As Watson explains: 'God commands nothing but what is beneficial. "O Israel, what doth the Lord require of thee, but to fear the Lord thy God, and to keep his statutes, which I command thee this day, for thy good." '[21] Obedience to God is not merely our duty but our privilege!

---

[20] Matthew 28.19–20.

[21] Quoted in I. D. E. Thomas, *op. cit.,* p. 199.

# Chapter 7

## *The Clearness Of Scripture*

*Psalm 119.129–136*

'Thy testimonies are wonderful: therefore doth my soul keep them. The entrance of thy words giveth light; it giveth understanding unto the simple. I opened my mouth, and panted: for I longed for thy commandments. Look thou upon me, and be merciful unto me, as thou usest to do unto those that love thy name. Order my steps in thy word: and let not any iniquity have dominion over me. Deliver me from the oppression of man: so will I keep thy precepts. Make thy face to shine upon thy servant; and teach me thy statutes. Rivers of waters run down mine eyes, because they keep not thy law.'

Sometimes as we read the Bible we come to a verse and we cannot understand the meaning. It might just be the words that we cannot understand because the scriptures are rich in vocabulary and many scriptural terms are unfamiliar in our culture. One example is the 'inkhorn.'[1] The biro has made the 'inkwell' redundant. Each pupil's desk had a hole cut at the top edge with its small porcelain pot to hold the ink for the school child's pen and nib. The inkhorn was a kind of mobile inkwell or pot sometimes attached to a writing board and some had the tube-like appearance of a cow's horn. Some used liquid ink and some ink cakes. Some learned scholar would be able to give a two-hour lecture on inkhorns. It is only one word out of the 8674 words in Strong's Hebrew and Chaldee Dictionary.[2] If you spent two hours each day on one Hebrew or Chaldee word it would take you twenty four years to get through all of the different words that are found in the Old Testament. A Bible word

---

[1] Ezekiel 9.2–3.

[2] James Strong, *The New Strong's Exhaustive Concordance of the Bible* (London: Thomas Nelson Publishers, 1990)

list, concordance or Bible Dictionary will give different levels of information but we cannot assume that any single English word will always be able to provide a full translation of a particular Hebrew word. The content of the word will still require explanation. However, the psalmist can say: 'The entrance of thy words giveth light; it giveth understanding unto the simple.' We thus need to consider: (1) The *perspicuity* of the scriptures, (2) *problems* in the scriptures and (3) *performing* the requirements of scripture.

## The *Perspicuity* of the Scriptures

The psalm is very clear: 'The entrance of thy words giveth light...' At first sight the word 'perspicuous' might seem to make things more complicated but specific words have exact meanings and if we want a particular meaning we have to use the appropriate word. The word *perspicuous* means 'clearly expressed'. It is something that is plain or obvious. The *No Smoking* sign is sufficiently plain that even children know what it means and what action is forbidden. The message is clear. Likewise the psalmist says that God's words go into the heart and they give light or understanding. As Charles Hodge comments: 'The Bible is a plain book. It is intelligible by the people. And they have the right, and are bound to read and interpret it for themselves; so that their faith may rest on the testimony of the Scriptures, and not on that of the Church.'[3] The Christian can say to his neighbour: 'You do not have to take my word for it. Go home and read the Bible for yourself.' The Bereans were a good example. Of them Luke states: 'These were more noble than those in Thessalonica, in that they received the word with all readiness of mind, and searched the scriptures daily, whether those things were so.'[4] The believer can be confident that the Bible is clear enough to show us Christ as the crucified Saviour, who died in a representative and substitutionary way to save sinners. The experience of every believer is that the Scriptures brought him or her to Christ as the Light of the World.

---

[3] Charles Hodge, *Systematic Theology, Volume I* (London: James Clarke & Co. Ltd., 1960) p. 183.
[4] Acts 17.11.

## *Problems* in the Scriptures

Of the Word of God the Psalm states: 'it giveth understanding unto the simple.' But, we might ask, can this really be correct? The *simple* will not know all of the ins and outs of the 'inkhorn' and what about all of the nuances of the other 8,673 words? The teaching of the Bible is that even the inexperienced, those who are not scholars, can make progress in understanding when the Holy Spirit is at work. This is well expressed in the following words of the Westminster Confession of Faith: 'All things in Scripture are not alike plain in themselves, nor alike clear unto all: yet those things which are necessary to be known, believed, and observed for salvation, are so clearly propounded and opened in some place of Scripture or other, that not only the learned, but the unlearned, in a due use of the ordinary means, may attain unto a sufficient understanding of them.'[5]

However, there are pitfalls for the proud and self-dependent who lean to their own understanding. Those who are spiritually unlearned trap themselves in darkness by trying to be wiser than what they are. So Peter warns of the danger of misinterpretation of the teaching of the Apostle Paul where there are passages that are difficult to understand. 'As also in all his epistles, speaking in them of these things; in which are some things hard to be understood, which they that are unlearned and unstable wrest, as they do also the other scriptures, unto their own destruction.'[6] And Paul likewise warns of those who are self-deceived: 'Now the end of the commandment is charity out of a pure heart, and of a good conscience, and of faith unfeigned: From which some having swerved have turned aside unto vain jangling; Desiring to be teachers of the law; understanding neither what they say, nor whereof they affirm.'[7] Such made the demand for *holiness* a demand for *merit* and changed the *evidence* of justification (a transformed life) into the *foundation* of justification; though *their* transformation was merely formal and ceremonial not spiritual.

---

[5] 'The Confession of Faith of the Westminster Assembly of Divines' Chapter 1.7 in S. W. Carruthers (ed.), *The Westminster Confession of Faith* (Manchester: R. Aikman & Son, 1937) p.92.

[6] 2 Peter 3.16.

[7] 1 Timothy 1.5–7.

Scripture does contain much that is *obscure*. We may think of the prophecies of Daniel or the Book of Revelation. We would be foolish to imagine that there are not things in these prophecies to exercise the greatest intellects. There are also in Scripture things that are *incomprehensible*. We are never going to fully understand them. We might think of the doctrine of the Trinity, the Incarnation and the Atonement. The Scripture reveals that there are three persons in the Godhead: God the Father, God the Son and God the Holy Spirit but we cannot fully understand the doctrine. The Apostle John tells us that the eternal Word was made flesh and dwelt among us but we cannot comprehend it. And when we are faced with the cross and the Saviour's cry: 'My God, my God, why hast thou forsaken me'[8] we cannot understand the extent of the agonies involved in his substitutionary sufferings to make peace by the blood of his cross.

However, though there is much that is obscure and incomprehensible it does not mean that what we need to know is hidden from us. The things that we need to know are clearly stated in one place or another and we do not need to be a scholar to understand them. We need only to use what the Confession describes as 'the ordinary means' to attain a sufficient understanding to be saved. These include: the prayerful reading of the scriptures; meditation upon the passages we read; the fellowship of the saints and consensus of the faithful to protect us from idiosyncrasies; and the exposition of the Word. We see the latter in the case of the Ethiopian Eunuch. 'And Philip ran thither to him, and heard him read the prophet Esaias, and said, Understandest thou what thou readest? And he said, How can I, except some man should guide me? And he desired Philip that he would come up and sit with him. The place of the scripture which he read was this, He was led as a sheep to the slaughter; and like a lamb dumb before his shearer, so opened he not his mouth: In his humiliation his judgment was taken away: and who shall declare his generation? for his life is taken from the earth. And the eunuch answered Philip, and said, I pray thee, of whom speaketh the prophet this? of himself, or of some other man? Then Philip opened his mouth, and began at the same scripture, and preached unto him Jesus.'[9] Philip was too wise an

---

[8] Psalm 22.1.
[9] Acts 8.30–35.

evangelist to leave this enquirer depending upon man's word; he began at the Scripture and preached to him Jesus who had come to save his people from their sins. 'That he was such a Saviour, and the very one predicted in the Hebrew Scriptures, was the doctrine now propounded and established in Philip's exegetical and argumentative discourse to his companion.'[10] Even the Saviour himself employed the same method. 'Then he said unto them, O fools, and slow of heart to believe all that the prophets have spoken: Ought not Christ to have suffered these things, and to enter into his glory? And beginning at Moses and all the prophets, *he expounded unto them in all the scriptures the things concerning himself.*'[11] Always the persuasion of the believer is to be based upon what the scriptures teach not upon the preacher or the Church.

## *Performing* the Requirements of Scripture

When we appreciate the value of the Scriptures we have a real desire to live by them. So the psalmist wrote: 'Thy testimonies are wonderful: therefore doth my soul keep them.'[12] *Performance* is the 'popular' word in management. How well does the manager perform? Does he meet his targets? Does he keep to his budgets? Does he come up to expectations? Does he match what he should be? So the psalmist is not only speaking about appreciation but action or performance. He says that God's testimonies are wonderful, that's *appreciation*; therefore he keeps the testimonies of God safely stored up in his heart; not as a hidden talent or pound, but as the directive force in his life leading to right *action*. If the heart is the dynamo that energizes us to godly action, the Word of God in the hand of the Holy Spirit is the power that drives the dynamo. Hence the prayer 'Order my steps in thy word: and let not any iniquity have dominion over me.'[13] When we fail to perform what is scriptural, our offence is not against man but against God. It is transgression. It is to allow the inroads of iniquity once again in our life as though sin had some claim upon us to have dominion over us, which it has not. God has

---

[10] J. A. Alexander, *A Commentary on The Acts of the Apostles* (Edinburgh: The Banner of Truth Trust, 1984) p.348.

[11] Luke 24.25–27.

[12] Verse 129.

[13] Verse 133.

given to us light for life and it is a shining *light* for a shining *life*! The light drives away the darkness. To change the metaphor: you may spend all your life and never find a vein of gold in the rock, but you will scarcely take a walk in the countryside and not find food around you. The Bible is like that. There are very deep seams of wisdom that are hard to exploit and found by few but at every hand and on every bush the genuine seeker will find food for his soul in Christ the living bread. How God urges us to partake of him and live! 'Ho, every one that thirsteth, come ye to the waters, and he that hath no money; come ye, buy, and eat; yea, come, buy wine and milk without money and without price. Wherefore do ye spend money for that which is not bread? and your labour for that which satisfieth not? hearken diligently unto me, and eat ye that which is good, and let your soul delight itself in fatness.'[14] Calvin's comment concerning this promise of God is apposite: 'Whoever shall submit to his word will have no reason to fear that he shall spend his strength on things of no value. Here we see the amazing goodness of God, who offers grace to men, though they are unthankful and unworthy.'[15]

---

[14] Isaiah 55.1–2

[15] John Calvin, *Commentary on the Book of the Prophet Isaiah, Volume IV* (Grand Rapids: Baker Book House, 2003) p. 159.

# Chapter 8

## *Scripture The Final Appeal*

*John 5.33–39*

'Ye sent unto John, and he bare witness unto the truth. But I receive not testimony from man: but these things I say, that ye might be saved. He was a burning and a shining light: and ye were willing for a season to rejoice in his light. But I have greater witness than that of John: for the works which the Father hath given me to finish, the same works that I do, bear witness of me, that the Father hath sent me. And the Father himself, which hath sent me, hath borne witness of me. Ye have neither heard his voice at any time, nor seen his shape. And ye have not his word abiding in you: for whom he hath sent, him ye believe not. Search the scriptures; for in them ye think ye have eternal life: and they are they which testify of me.'

No one had a more reverent esteem for the scriptures than the Lord Jesus Christ. He who was perfectly holy and had a perfect love for God the Father viewed the Old Testament as *the* witness to himself. He had the witness of John, the witness of his own works and the witness of his Father (verses 33–37), but he could still point the Jews to their 'Bible' as the permanent record concerning himself (verse 39). The context of Jesus' reference to the scriptures was the terrible ecclesiastical resistance to Christ and persecution of Christ. 'And therefore did the Jews persecute Jesus, and sought to slay him, because he had done these things on the sabbath day. But Jesus answered them, My Father worketh hitherto, and I work. Therefore the Jews sought the more to kill him, because he not only had broken the sabbath, but said also that God was his Father, making himself equal with God.'[1] Notwithstanding, Jesus made such stupendous claims concerning himself. 'Verily, verily, I say unto you, He

---

[1] John 5.16–18.

that heareth my word, and believeth on him that sent me, hath everlasting life, and shall not come into condemnation; but is passed from death unto life.'[2] Such a claim is surely worth examination? Jesus claimed to have the answer to death and the gift of eternal life! But who is right, Jesus or the Jews? The question is raised: *How* is the religious dispute to be settled? What is Jesus' answer? 'Use your Bible.' This leads us to consider (1) the *authenticity* of the scriptures as the Word of God written, (2) our *access* to the scriptures as the Word of God and (3) the *abiding* of God's Word in us.

## The *Authenticity* of the Scriptures as the Word of God

In the words *search the scriptures* our Lord made reference to the Word of God written as the last word on the matter, the ultimate authority and final court of appeal. It used to be the case in Britain that once the House of Lords had settled a legal matter that was the end of it. Now the British must go elsewhere to the European Court but there always has to be some point of *final* reference. If we go only to the Magistrates' Court we will not get the highest authority on a matter and things might not be as they seem. We go ahead thinking that we have covered our position but then further legal action is taken and a higher authority says, 'No, the magistrate was wrong!' Sometimes in the affairs of men the court itself is just a sham and its pronouncements are worthless. John Bunyan depicts such a scene in *Vanity Fair* when *Envy* gives his evidence against the believer: 'I heard him once... affirm, *That Christianity and the Customs of our Town of* Vanity, *were Diametrically opposite, and could not be reconciled.* By which saying, my Lord, he doth at once, not only condemn all our laudable doings, but us in the doing of them.' *Pickthank* added that he 'hath spoke contemptibly of... honourable Friends, whose names are the Lord *Oldman*, the Lord *Carnal-delight*, the Lord *Luxurious*, the Lord *Desire of Vain-glory*, my old Lord *Lechery*, Sir *Having Greedy*, with all the rest of our Nobility.'[3] However, by the ultimate standards of God the believing testimony thus censured was not worthy of condemnation but was praiseworthy.

---

[2] John 5.24.

[3] John Bunyan, *The Pilgrim's Progress* (London: Henry Frowde, 1904) pp. 115–116.

Clearly a start must be made with the right standard. The counterfeiter robs us; his notes are not authentic, they are not according to the sovereign's standard. Where then is the reliable and ultimate standard for moral and spiritual things? The Westminster Confession states matters as follows: 'The Old Testament in Hebrew (which was the native language of the people of God of old), and the New Testament in Greek (which, at the time of the writing of it was most generally known to the nations), being immediately inspired by God, and, by His singular care and providence kept pure in all ages, are therefore authentical; so as, in all controversies of religion, the Church is finally to appeal unto them.'[4] This is not the *final appeal* in the sense of *last*, when having tried everything else we have found all others to fail, which will be the case, but *final* in the sense of *beyond which* we are not to seek to go. We are not to turn to the traditions of men, unaided human reason or the philosophies of this world. You see Christ's method. There is a God-breathed word, which has been kept by his invincible providence, and which, being in our hands in faithful transcripts, is to be consulted.

## Our *Access* to the Scriptures as the Word of God

The Saviour's prescribed method is to search the scriptures. He says, *'Search the scriptures,'* as writings which you have to hand; he does not say 'Search *for* the scriptures' as writings that are lost and need to be recovered. We *have* the authentic Word of God but there is still a difficulty. To search with understanding we must be able to read the scriptures but most cannot consult the Hebrew and the Greek originals being ignorant of the ancient languages. In the Gospel Church many believers would understand the Septuagint version translated at Alexandria in the third century BC from the Hebrew into Greek. It was useful and generally reliable and is apparently quoted in the New Testament but it is the original Hebrew which is the ultimate authority. It is clear from the New Testament that the unlearned or common people are expected to search the scriptures and the Bereans were commended

---

[4] 'The Confession of Faith of the Westminster Assembly of Divines' Chapter 1.8 in S. W. Carruthers (ed.), *The Westminster Confession of Faith* (Manchester: R. Aikman & Son, 1937) p. 92.

for this.[5] The believer must prove for himself what he has been taught. He must be persuaded of the truth on the authority of God's Word. This was what the believers at Thessalonica had to do and Paul was glad of it: 'For this cause also thank we God without ceasing, because, when ye received the word of God which ye heard of us, ye received it not as the word of men, but as it is in truth, the word of God, which effectually worketh also in you that believe.'[6]

The Church needs reliable scholarly ministers with true theological insight to refer to the original languages but we must also have the Word of God in the *vulgar language* or *vernacular* for all to read. Therefore the Confession goes on to state: 'But, because these original tongues are not known to all the people of God, who have right unto, and interest in the Scriptures, and are commanded, in the fear of God, to read and search them, therefore they are to be translated into the vulgar language of every nation unto which they come, that the Word of God dwelling plentifully in all, they may worship Him in an acceptable manner; and, through patience and comfort of the Scriptures, may have hope.'[7] The expression *in the fear of God* is noteworthy. Many these days are full of criticism of the Authorised (King James) Version but without just cause. This English translation serves the needs of God-fearing people because it was translated by God-fearing men with a firm theological grasp of what the scriptures teach and who had a reverence for the Word of God as it has come down to us.

### The *Abiding* of the Word of God in Us

However accessible the Word of God might be, even if regularly heard and read, it is of no personal spiritual profit unless it *abides* in our *hearts*. The Jews had the scriptures but of them the Saviour clearly states: 'And ye have not his word abiding in you: for whom he hath sent, him ye believe not' (verse 38). Paul thus extols their great *privilege*: 'What

---

[5] Acts 17.11

[6] 1 Thessalonians 2.13.

[7] 'The Confession of Faith of the Westminster Assembly of Divines' Chapter 1.8 in S. W. Carruthers (ed.), *The Westminster Confession of Faith* (Manchester: R. Aikman & Son, 1937) p. 92

advantage then hath the Jew? or what profit is there of circumcision? Much every way: chiefly, because that unto them were committed the oracles of God.'[8] How sad that they did not appreciate it. The word was not *abiding* in them. How we should appreciate the Scripture, God's Word written, and love it! When the word abides in the heart the believing soul experiences eternal life. The connection that the Jews made between the Scripture and eternal life was not mistaken. The problem was that the Word did not find a lodging place in their hearts. They needed to heed the exhortation the Saviour gave to the Laodiceans: 'Behold, I stand at the door, and knock: if any man hear my voice, and open the door, I will come in to him, and will sup with him, and he with me.'[9] We must receive the word as the voice of Christ and hear, believe and obey. When we do so, it is the Living Word himself that we know in our hearts, 'Christ in you, the hope of glory.'[10] *He with me.* This abiding of the word in our hearts is soul transforming as the Confession explains: 'translated … *that* the Word of God dwelling plentifully in all, *they may worship Him in an acceptable manner; and, through patience and comfort of the Scriptures, may have hope.*' This follows the words of the Apostle: 'For whatsoever things were written aforetime were written for our learning, that we through patience and comfort of the scriptures might have hope.'[11]

When someone is precious to you, you keep his letters. When he is far away you read the letters again and again and they bring your loved one near, right into your heart. The faithful soldier's wife knows that. He is precious to her. His letters are eagerly awaited and carefully read. She ponders every word. Christian, how you should read the Bible like that; for shall the Church deal with Christ who bought her with less love than many a bride?

---

[8] Romans 3.1–2.
[9] Revelation 3.20.
[10] Colossians 1.27.
[11] Romans 15.4.

# Chapter 9

## The Text Of Scripture: The Originals And Their Transmission

*The Authentic Text – Textual Transmission*

### THE AUTHENTIC TEXT

As we have seen Paragraph 8 of Chapter 1 of the Westminster Confession deals with the subject of the authenticity of the Old and New Testaments in the original languages, their final authority in controversies of religion and the need for translations. The words, as we saw, are as follows:

> 'The Old Testament in Hebrew (which was the native language of the people of God of old), and the New Testament in Greek (which, at the time of the writing of it was most generally known to the nations), being immediately inspired by God, and, by His singular care and providence kept pure in all ages, are therefore authentic; so as, in all controversies of religion, the Church is finally to appeal unto them. But, because these original tongues are not known to all the people of God, who have right unto, and interest in the Scriptures, and are commanded, in the fear of God, to read and search them, therefore they are to be translated into the vulgar language of every nation unto which they come, that the Word of God dwelling plentifully in all, they may worship Him in an acceptable manner; and, through patience and comfort of the Scriptures, may have hope.'[1]

---

[1] 'The Confession of Faith of the Westminster Assembly of Divines' Chapter 1.8 in S. W. Carruthers (ed.), *The Westminster Confession of Faith* (Manchester: R. Aikman & Son, 1937) p.92. The appended Scripture references are Matthew 5.18; Isaiah 8.20; Acts 15.15; John 5.39, 46; John 5.39; I Corinthians 14.6, 9, 11, 12, 24, 27, 28; Colossians 3.16 and Rom 15.4.

It will be clear to the reader that this is a very important subject bearing upon the reliability of the Scripture texts and translations that we use. It will help us to better understand the important issues involved to consider the words of the Lord Jesus Christ as they are recorded in John 10.34–36.

### *John 10.34–36*

'Jesus answered them, Is it not written in your law, I said, Ye are gods? If he called them gods, unto whom the word of God came, and the scripture cannot be broken; Say ye of him, whom the Father hath sanctified, and sent into the world, Thou blasphemest; because I said, I am the Son of God?'

The question: Who is Jesus? demands an answer and many blasphemous suggestions have been given. Some regard him as a Jewish monk and others regard him as a superstar. To the Jehovah's Witnesses he is a created angel and to the Mormons a polygamist. Heresies with respect to Jesus are not new. The Apostle John wrote his Gospel against the background of the First Century philosophical 'Logos' that was thought to serve as a bridge between God and the World. However, the Apostle began with the astonishing truth of the Incarnation: 'In the beginning was the Word, and the Word was with God, and the Word was God... And the Word was made flesh, and dwelt among us, (and we beheld his glory, the glory as of the only begotten of the Father,) full of grace and truth.'[2] It was none other than the eternal Son of God who had come in the flesh and was known by men: 'That which was from the beginning, which we have heard, which we have seen with our eyes, which we have looked upon, and our hands have handled, of the Word of life; (For the life was manifested, and we have seen it, and bear witness, and shew unto you that eternal life, which was with the Father, and was manifested unto us;) That which we have seen and heard declare we unto you, that ye also

---

[2] John 1.1,14.

may have fellowship with us: and truly our fellowship is with the Father, and with his Son Jesus Christ.'[3]

It was equally astonishing that he the *Living* Word should place such honour upon the *written* Word as to rest his case upon it, saying, 'Is it not *written* in your law…?' Surely this will humble us to a reverent approach to the Bible especially concerning its reliability? Of the written Word Jesus could say: 'The scripture cannot be broken.' We cannot say that of the word of politicians, doctors, lawyers, teachers or scientists because all make mistakes and get things wrong at times. But we can have confidence in the Old and New Testaments (1) because of *what* the Bible is, (2) because of this *word* of Jesus about it and (3) because of the *way* in which the Lord used it as an utterly reliable witness.

## We can have Confidence in the Bible because of *What* it is

In verses 34 and 35 quoted above we have three fundamental descriptions of the sacred text. The Lord Jesus Christ endorses it as 'your law', 'the word of God' and 'the scripture'.

### Your Law

The customary threefold division of the Old Testament was referred to by our Lord: 'And he said unto them, These are the words which I spake unto you, while I was yet with you, that all things must be fulfilled, which were written in the law of Moses, and in the prophets, and in the psalms, concerning me.'[4] But the quotation we are dealing with is from Psalm 82.6 and not from 'the Law'. Why then is it referred to as 'Law'? It is helpful to remember in this connection that Genesis 1–50, Exodus 1–18, nineteen chapters of Numbers and the first four chapters of Deuteronomy are history. Thus ninety-one of the one hundred and eighty seven chapters of the Pentateuch are *history*. 'The Law' is thus fifty percent history! This helps us to understand that 'Law', in the context in John, is emphasizing, not merely commandments, but *binding authority*. Thus we find Isaiah saying: 'And when they shall say unto you, Seek unto them that have familiar spirits, and unto wizards that peep, and that

---

[3] 1 John 1.1–3.
[4] Luke 24.44.

mutter: should not a people seek unto their God? for the living to the dead? *To the law and to the testimony: if they speak not according to this word, it is because there is no light in them.*[5] The Bible must then have the last word (and the first word) because it is the *only* word of God written.

## The Word of God

'The Word of God' points us to the origin of the Bible. Its Author is God. Thus the Saviour in repelling the Devil stated: 'It is written, Man shall not live by bread alone, but by *every word that proceedeth out of the mouth of God.*'[6] But was not the Bible written by men? Yes, indeed! But the men were men carried along by the Spirit of God so that, without reducing them to robots, what they *wrote* was what God *spoke*. 'For the prophecy came not in old time by the will of man: but holy men of God spake as they were moved by the Holy Ghost.'[7] The *process* is a mystery but not the *product*. The Bible is a God-breathed word. It is His Word. Thus the Apostle's confidence in it: 'All scripture is given by inspiration of God, *and is profitable* for doctrine, for reproof, for correction, for instruction in righteousness: That the man of God may be perfect, *throughly furnished* unto all good works.'[8] The Apostolic faith is that David spoke but the word was God's word: 'And when they heard that, they lifted up their voice to God with one accord, and said, Lord, thou art God, which hast made heaven, and earth, and the sea, and all that in them is: *Who by the mouth of thy servant David hast said*, Why did the heathen rage, and the people imagine vain things?'[9]

## The Scripture

'The Scripture' points to the Bible as the Word of God *written*. When, in my school days, the teacher said: 'You have a nice *script*' it was equivalent to her saying that you had good *writing*. When Jesus said, "Is

---

[5] Isaiah 8.19–20.

[6] Matthew 4.4.

[7] 2 Peter 1.21.

[8] 2 Timothy 3.16–17.

[9] Acts 4.24–25.

it not *written* in your law?" he was not appealing to some oral tradition. This is not something depending upon recollection of what your teachers have said. Is it not *written*? How often you have wished that you wrote down the contents of that telephone call. What time was the meeting? Which hospital ward were you supposed to be visiting? We are not left to recollect what men said about what God said. We are able to read what God said. We have his word in permanent form! This Peter states is more sure than the voice of God from heaven in this respect: 'And this voice which came from heaven we heard, when we were with him in the holy mount. *We have also a more sure word of prophecy*; whereunto ye do well that ye take heed, as unto a light that shineth in a dark place, until the day dawn, and the day star arise in your hearts: Knowing this first, that *no prophecy of the scripture* is of any private interpretation...'[10] With regard to the Scripture its authority is absolute, its originator is God and its form is permanent. We can have absolute confidence in it.

### We can have Confidence in the Bible because of this *Word* of the Lord Jesus

Jesus states that 'the scripture *cannot be broken*.' In so saying the Lord is not referring to the manuscript in David's handwriting. When he asks: 'Is it not written in your law' he is referring to the manuscripts to which they had access in their generation. The original Greek translated 'written' is the perfect passive participle indicating: once written so that you have it *now*. It is a reference to something accomplished that has resulted in continuing effects right up to their own time. The reference can only be to the scriptures in the Temple, in their synagogues and in their studies; the God-breathed and God-preserved authoritative Word of the Lord that endures forever to which they had access.

This preserved scripture is reliable *to a word*. The Saviour's argument hinges upon the one word 'gods'. We have the same in Galatians 3.16: 'Now to Abraham and his seed were the promises made. He saith not, And to *seeds*, as of many; but as of one, And to thy *seed*, which is Christ.' The apostle's argument rests upon a single word. The scriptures in the original languages have been transmitted in such a degree of purity

---

[10] 2 Peter 1.18–20.

as to make the appeal to a single word possible. The Lord believed that a single word 'gods' could be decisive in his debate with the Jews. The originals in our hands thus have *verbal* authenticity and whatever difficulties are presented by the existence of variants between manuscripts they must not be allowed to detract from this fact. We cannot accept that variant readings impinge upon the verbal accuracy of *Scripture* because the divergent readings are no part of Scripture. Our Reformers were not ignorant scholars and were aware of variants. They discussed them on a case by case basis as their writings show; but they would not allow the Sectarian attempts and the Romanist attempts to lessen the authority of the Scripture in our hands because some variants exist. Christ says that the Scripture in our hands cannot be broken and this is true wherever faithful transmission has taken place. Thus concerning the Scripture William Hendriksen comments: 'It is absolutely indestructible, no matter how man may regard it. The Old Testament, *as it lies there in written form!* is inspired, infallible, authoritative.'[11]

We must, therefore, reject the idea that the Church had a *corrupted* text of Scripture until the nineteenth century. The assumption is unscriptural and no theory of textual criticism can be relied upon that involves the denial of the scriptural truth that God has preserved his Word, in the hands of his church, through the centuries; unbreakable down to a single word. This is our Lord's doctrine. We are not to imagine that some manuscripts will be discovered that will show that all this time the church has been relying upon an imperfect and corrupted textual tradition. Our Lord's teaching involves the acceptance of the reliability of the sacred text as we have it in the ecclesiastically transmitted text. The Saviour's words at this point are crucial for a right understanding of the place of the originals and the extant copies of them in the life of the Church. The Lord states: 'The *scripture* cannot be broken.' He did not say: 'the immediately inspired *autographs* cannot be broken' because he was not referring merely to them. He was referring to the ecclesiastically transmitted texts extant at the time that men could turn to and read. Christ does not hesitate to call these Hebrew manuscripts or scrolls 'the *scripture*.' In the mind of Christ there was no disconnection between

---

[11] William Hendriksen, *The Gospel of John* (Edinburgh: The Banner of Truth Trust, 1969) p.128.

immediately inspired autographs and the copies by uninspired men which witnessed to them. Rather he refers to *a providentially preserved, immediately inspired Word of God written* that could be regarded as the final authority for settling disputes. The Westminster Confession in its specification of the Reformed doctrine of Scripture was extremely careful to maintain this integrated articulation. As we have seen it stated: 'The Old Testament in Hebrew..., and the New Testament in Greek..., being immediately inspired by God, and, by His singular care and providence kept pure in all ages, are therefore authentical...' The present tense is to be noted: The Old Testament in Hebrew and the New Testament in Greek *are* authentical. They are authentical as a result of two things: (1) being immediately inspired by God and (2) being kept pure in all ages by God's singular care and providence. This exactly replicates the doctrine of Christ who could say: 'search the scriptures'[12] a statement that would have no practical meaning if it did not apply to the manuscripts in their hands to which they could refer. He does not say: 'search *for* the scriptures,' among the existing Hebrew scrolls at your disposal; as though there was some problem that the manuscript witnesses to the original autographs were so inadequate that they must search around among them to *find* the Word of God! The doctrine of the Saviour was that the Jewish Church *had* the scriptures. We can only conclude from this that his understanding of the situation was that the providence of God had so superintended the *ecclesiastical transmission* of the text of Scripture that the immediately inspired Word of God had come down to his generation in its purity.

The scholastic construction is not consistent with this scriptural doctrine of the preservation of the text. It approaches the situation in a different way maintaining that the inspired autographs having been *lost*, the Church was left only with corrupted texts until the discovery of older manuscripts and the development of 'scientific' methods of textual criticism enabled contemporary academics to reconstruct a closer approximation to the autographs from extant manuscript witnesses. This construction is not faithful to our Lord's teaching.

---

[12] John 5.39.

**We can have Confidence in the Bible because of the *Way* in which our Lord used it**

The example of the Lord was to apply the Sacred Text to matters of dispute and to do so in a way which recognized not only the *authority* of the scriptures as the final word in settling controversies but also their *inviolability* as incapable of error. Thus he states: 'If he called them gods, unto whom the word of God came, *and the scripture cannot be broken*; Say ye of him, whom the Father hath sanctified, and sent into the world, Thou blasphemest; because I said, I am the Son of God?' In pursuing his argument, it would be enough to demonstrate that its basis was scriptural. Once this was done his case was established because there is no possibility of the scriptures being found wanting or their testimony being faulted in any way.

## TEXTUAL TRANSMISSION

It is necessary to address the subject of the transmission of the text because it has become a means of undermining confidence in the Holy Scriptures. Contrary to our Lord's example an undue emphasis has been placed upon the distinction between the *autographs* written by the inspired human authors under the superintendence of the Holy Spirit and the *apographa* which have been copied from them under the superintendence of Divine providence. We have noted above that the Lord Jesus Christ did not see this distinction as being of any significance in connection with the authenticity of the Old Testament in the hands of the Jews of his own day. As we have seen, he said to the Jews *search the scriptures*, referring to something in their possession; not *search* for *the scriptures*, as something lost and needing to be recovered. This is decisive for our understanding of the transmission of the text and it is important to state our position as an outflow from scriptural principles and not as a reaction to issues. Wrong answers often arise as a result of the way in which questions are posed and we must avoid being drawn onto alien territory by a genuine desire to answer every man's complaints. Thus in view of our Lord's approach to Scripture we do not start from the assumption that the *autographs* were perfect and the *apographa* are corrupted so that we now need to recover the authentic word. Rather it is necessary for the scriptural logic of our position to be stated in a way that does full justice to our Lord's presuppositions.

In relation to Holy Scripture there are four levels of activity: (1) its being written, (2) its being copied, (3) its translation and (4) its interpretation. The distinctions and relationships between these four activities are important. The Reformed view of Scripture as set out in such documents as the Westminster Confession of Faith, the Baptist Confession 1689 and the Savoy Declaration of the Congregationalists is clear. These confessions define Scripture as the Word of God written, given by inspiration of God and consequently infallible, authoritative for faith and life and comprised of the 39 books of the Old Testament together with the 27 books of the New Testament. This definition applies to scripture whether (1) in the autographs, (2) in copies or (3) in translations. It does not apply to the commentaries of men providing (4) the interpretation of scripture. Additionally we must understand that certain caveats are necessary with respect to copies and translations, as we shall see.

## The Autographs

The autographs are distinguished by the fact that the prophets, apostles and others through whom the revelation was communicated were under the direct control of the Holy Spirit in such a way that not a single word was written other than what the Holy Spirit intended. The *process* is usually described as 'inspiration' and the *product* (or writing produced) is described as 'inspired' or God-breathed. When we refer to extant (existing) copies of the scriptures as 'inspired' we do not mean that those who did the copying were under the direct control of the Holy Spirit in the way in which the original human authors were: but only that the words of the copy are the God-breathed words originally communicated and that therefore the copy *is* the inspired Word of God. This requires more explanation.

## Copies of the Scripture in the Original Hebrew and Greek

The original languages of the scriptures were Hebrew and Greek and copies of the scriptures in these languages are the infallible Scripture. When the Lord Jesus Christ said: 'Search the scriptures; for in them ye think ye have eternal life: and they are they which testify of me'[13] his

---

[13] John 5.39.

words, as we have seen, could only have meaning in relation to extant manuscripts (the *then existing copies*) of the Old Testament. The activity of copying the inerrant scripture does not and never did require that those who copy should be borne along by the Holy Spirit in the way that the human *authors* of the scripture were. Copies arise, not from the writing of the text by the human authors under such direction of the Holy Spirit, but from its transmission. Transmission in itself requires no subjective judgments of fallible men. The task is merely one of copying what is there and the faithful copyist reproduced what he found before him. Individual copyists were not, however, infallible and consequently circumstances could have arisen which required the most faithful of copyists to exercise a measure of subjective judgment. The document being copied may have been illegible at some point and in order to complete the text another document would have to be referred to. Perhaps two were available with varying readings. The copyist would then have to choose between the alternative readings. There was thus the possibility of the choice of a correct or incorrect reading. In the event of an incorrect reading being chosen the copy would still be a copy of the inerrant scripture but containing a *copying* variant. Because of the variant the manuscript would not be a *perfect copy* but as far as the manuscript *is* infallible scripture the copy would be reliable.

Variant readings have not deprived the Church of the Scripture because mistakes in one copy can be corrected by correct readings in others. The genuine text has been in the hands of the Church in the multitude of copies. We have noted the use of the present tense in the Westminster Confession of Faith: 'The Old Testament in Hebrew... and the New Testament in Greek... being immediately inspired by God, and, by His singular care and providence, kept pure in all ages, *are therefore authentical*; so as, in all controversies of religion, the Church is finally to appeal to them...'[14] This is a reference to the scriptures in the original languages *in the hands of the Church*. They *are* (present tense) authentical. It is the responsibility of the Church to use the most reliable copies at its disposal, as there is a spectrum of reliability and some copies

---

[14] 'The Confession of Faith of the Westminster Assembly of Divines' Chapter 1.8 in S. W. Carruthers (ed.), *The Westminster Confession of Faith* (Manchester: R. Aikman & Son, 1937) p.92.

of the scripture outside of the main strand of transmission *have* been corrupted. Some manuscripts even contradict the fundamental nature of scripture as infallible because they contain readings that require us to conclude that the *original writers* made mistakes. So, for example, those texts, which read 'Amos' instead of 'Amon'[15] by *their* mistake, deny that Scripture *as originally given* through Matthew was free from error. Such copies cannot be regarded as reliable and have always been and are unsuitable for normal ecclesiastical use.

God's providential preservation of the text of Scripture in the original Hebrew and the original Greek is not inconsistent with variants in particular manuscripts. These variants do not, however, deprive the Church of the infallible and error-free Scripture because it is contained in the multitude of copies. To affirm that a particular single copy is a *reliable* witness it is not necessary to affirm that it is a *perfectly* verbatim copy. It is the responsibility of the Church to transmit copies of the scripture and in so doing to use the most reliable copies available. In relation to this any acceptable method of textual criticism must *increase* the certainty as to what is the infallible scripture. Methods that increase the uncertainty as to what is the text of the infallible and error-free Scripture are not suitable methods. It is for this reason that the eclectic texts of the Nineteenth Century onwards are not a satisfactory approach. Jakob Van Bruggen comments upon them as follows: 'In modern textual criticism the eclectic method is generally followed: per *reading* a decision is made on the basis of a complicated structure of considerations. Subjectivity is not out of the question with this method. Thus they will just have to arrive at a text by majority-vote. Nobody is happy with this. However nobody also dares to state that there is already sufficient certainty to do it differently. Thus the agreement concerning the text-*edition* to be used camouflages the uncertainty which prevails during the *fixation* of the text.'[16]

It has been mentioned already that some copies contradict the fundamental nature of scripture as infallible and free from error, where

---

[15] Matthew 1.10

[16] Jakob van Bruggen, *The Ancient Text of the New Testament* (Winnipeg, Manitoba: Premier, 1979) pp. 10–11.

readings contained would require us to conclude that the *original writers* made mistakes. Such copies are unreliable and unsuitable for normal ecclesiastical use and should not be accorded determinative status in textual criticism. Decisions regarding preferred readings within a reliable textual tradition require appropriate competence and the pastors and teachers of the Church have responsibility to express their considered view on a case by case basis as necessary. This follows the example set within the Reformed community. Major textual matters involve theological interpretation as well as manuscript evidence and cannot be left to unbelieving textual critics. In choosing a particular text to underlie its work a Bible Society does not thereby accord a status to the copy that is only applicable to the original manuscripts. The status of an adopted text is that of a reliable copy of inerrant scripture but the claim is not thereby made for that particular copy that it is *perfect* in the way in which the original manuscripts were. It is regarded as a copy of very high quality that has been recognized as such by successive generations of ministers and Christians.

As we have seen the teaching of Christ precludes the idea that the Jewish Church had a corrupted Old Testament and the English Protestant confessions in following the Saviour reject the idea that the Church has had for centuries a corrupted Bible and that only in recent time have scholars been able to recover the uncorrupted text. Our seventeenth century confessions explicitly assert the preservation of an accurate text of the Bible in accordance with our Lord's expressed confidence on this point: 'Till heaven and earth pass, one jot or one tittle shall in no wise pass from the law, till all be fulfilled.'[17] Although the Lord frequently reproved the scribes and Pharisees for setting aside the Word of God by their human traditions he did not accuse them of corrupting the scriptural records themselves. Indeed it is inconceivable that God should give His Word in written form for the comfort of His Church and then fail to preserve that Word from generation to generation. Consequently, Presbyterians, Congregationalists and Baptists have all confessed God-breathed autographs, accurate transmission of their text and the need for translations.

---

[17] Matthew 5.18.

However, much attention has been given to the distinction between the *autographa* written by prophets and apostles and the *apographa* or copies. The former, as we have seen, were written by holy men of God under the inspiration of the Holy Spirit and thus were kept completely free from any error. Copies of the *autographa* and copies of the copies have since been made and this transmission of the text has taken place over the centuries. It might be assumed that the Scripture we have now is greatly departed from what was originally written but the transmission of the text was under the providential oversight of God and consequently His Word written, as a matter of fact, has been kept pure in all ages. This is not to assert that every copy is an exact replica, which clearly is not the case, because variant readings do exist; rather, it is to state that *at no time has God allowed His Word to lose its authenticity*. The case is well stated with respect to the Old Testament by Eugene H. Merrill in *An Historical Survey of the Old Testament*: 'As more and more copies were made and a multitude of translations were produced it is easy to understand that slight differences in the texts began to appear, especially if the copying and translating were done by individuals who did not carefully enough ensure against copying errors. As a result, the manuscripts which have survived down to the present day, representing many Hebrew text traditions as well as numerous ancient translations and versions, do not agree in every single point. Yet, it is remarkable to note that even those texts which vary most do so in matters of very little importance, and certainly it is safe to say that their differences are of no theological or doctrinal moment whatsoever. Furthermore, those texts which vary most from the Hebrew *textus receptus* (received text) are not regarded by the scholars as possessing much independent authority on the whole, so the differences are even more minimized.'[18]

Merrill explains that the Dead Sea Scrolls moved our access to the Hebrew text from the tenth century AD back one thousand years, in some cases to 150 BC. He continues: 'And to the delight of those who had all along maintained the integrity of the modern Hebrew text, those of

---

[18] Eugene H. Merrill, *An Historical Survey of the Old Testament* (Nutley, New Jersey: The Craig Press, 1975) p.12. Merrill's endnote at this point is to D. Winton Thomas, 'The Textual Criticism of the Old Testament,' *The Old Testament and Modern Study*, ed. H. H. Rowley (Oxford: Clarendon Press, 1951) pp. 244–245.

Qumran were in the majority of the cases essentially the same. The major differences (mostly in Samuel and Kings) can be accounted for by recognizing that in some cases the scribes at Qumran had preferred the Septuagint, or Greek, version, over the Hebrew, but this by no means proves that the Septuagint was the more accurate reflection of the originals as written by the Bible writers.

'In short, it is safe to say without hesitation that we possess the originals insofar as they were faithfully preserved by godly and exacting scribes down through the ages. It is not overstating the case to say that we possess the Old Testament of the prophets. This is only as it must be, for it is theologically inconceivable to believe that God who inspired the original manuscripts would permit them to lose their value as inerrant revelation by failing to preserve them. The very inspiration of the Old Testament assures its faithful textual preservation.'[19]

Robert Shaw explains the position with respect to the New Testament in his book entitled *The Reformed Faith: An exposition of the Confession of Faith of the Westminster Assembly of Divines*. He states: 'The corruption of the books of the New Testament is altogether incredible. Had any party entertained a wish to alter them, it would have been impossible for them to succeed. Copies were speedily multiplied; they were early translated into the different languages of the several nations among which the gospel was planted; the Christian fathers embodied numerous quotations from them into their writings; various sects soon arose, keenly opposed to each other, but all receiving the same sacred books, and these became a check upon each other, and rendered corruptions and interpolations impracticable. Every succeeding age increased the difficulty; and though the comparison of a multitude of ancient manuscripts and copies has discovered a vast number of various readings, occasioned by the inadvertency and inaccuracy of transcribers, yet none of these differences affect any one article of the faith and comfort of Christians.'[20]

---

[19] *Ibid.*, pp. 12–13. Merrill's endnote at this point is to F. F. Bruce, *Second Thoughts on the Dead Sea Scrolls* (Grand Rapids: Wm B. Eerdmans Publishing Company, 1964) p. 96.

[20] Robert Shaw, *The Reformed Faith: An Exposition of the Confession of Faith of the Westminster Assembly of Divines* (Inverness: Christian Focus Publications, 1973) p.21.

This raises the question as to which is the text that God has kept pure 'in all ages'? On the basis of what we have already said about our Lord's doctrine of Scripture it can only be that text which has been in common use in His Church under the control of a hearing people who, knowing the Scripture, were consequently capable of identifying unreliable copies by the spurious readings contained. With respect to the New Testament this text has come down to us under the name of the *Byzantine Tradition* of which the '*Received Text*' is the most familiar representative. It should not surprise us that early copies of this textual tradition are no longer extant, as, long ago, they will have been worn out by frequent use. We can be confident, however, that accurate copies of accurate copies are reliable copies; and that such copies can be more reliable than older copies made from poorer manuscripts.

# Chapter 10

# *Textual Criticism, Translation And Interpretation*

*Textual Criticism – Translations – Interpretation*

## TEXTUAL CRITICISM

What has been discussed in the previous chapter leads us to consider the significance of textual criticism. Variant readings do exist, even within the Byzantine tradition, and the framers of the Westminster Confession were not ignorant of this. Indeed they were aware that both Romanism and the sectaries appealed to variant readings to undermine the authority of Scripture, the former to maintain the necessity of an infallible Church to confirm what is truth and the latter to set aside the responsibility of being in submission to Scripture. In connection with the New Testament, the translators of the Authorized Version used several different texts as well as the Latin Vulgate and Tyndale's English. Scrivener lists the following: the Complutensian N.T., Erasmus, Aldus, Colinaeus, Stephanus, and the Antwerp Polyglott, 1572 as sources for the Authorized Version in addition to Beza's New Testament of 1598.[1] Thus the confessional position need not be interpreted as arguing for the infallibility of any particular manuscript of the Received Text tradition.

However, it is important to remember that a century of intense textual criticism has left untouched ninety five per cent of the Received Text. Of the remaining five per cent or so, many of the variants are of a very minor nature such as 'Christ Jesus' instead of 'Jesus Christ' in 1 Timothy 1.1. There are, however, a number of passages where the Received Text has been challenged on the basis of 'textual criticism' and where the variations are more significant. We, therefore, need to examine whether or not the current enthusiasm for the neo-Westcott and Hort

---

[1] F. H. A. Scrivener, *The New Testament in the Original Greek According to the Text followed in the Authorised Version together with the Variations Adopted in the Revised Version* (Cambridge: University Press, 1881) p. 648.

theory of textual criticism is well founded and consequently deserving of the credit accorded to it by conservative evangelical scholars. And, in addition, we need to examine whether the application of such a theory of textual criticism should be permitted to determine the content of translations of the Scripture in circulation in evangelical Churches.

The first point that needs to be made is in connection with the results of the transmission of the text of Scripture as it has come down to us in the providence of God. For the New Testament we have at our disposal over a thousand cursive manuscripts and a handful of ancient uncials.[2] These are all objective historical documents, in substantial agreement with one another most of the time but with some significant variations. An accurate translation of any one of these documents would faithfully transmit in the vernacular the text of that particular witness to the original autographs. However, there are also theories of textual criticism. The latter is rightly regarded as an art as well as a science, involving a subjective element, which is by no means an insignificant factor. Different scholars evaluate the available evidence and come to different conclusions. Consequently, a translation of an eclectic text, which is built out of such textual criticism, never faithfully transmits any historical or providential witness to the original autographs of Scripture. Rather, it transmits the subjective opinions of the scholars at the time of compilation as to what is the authentic text. It is for this reason that the translation of an historical document which has come down to us in the providence of God, plus, if desired, footnotes concerning contemporary judgements about the text, based upon objective and subjective considerations, represents a more faithful transmission of the text in the common tongue. Some may prefer to take one of the more ancient uncial manuscripts, others a representative document within the Byzantine tradition, but both would be transmitting in translation an historical text given to us in the providence of God. Its overall quality could then be judged by the people of God and the translation and its underlying text accepted or rejected. In this case rejection would be in total, as a

---

[2] Kurt Aland provided a total figure of 5,255 known manuscripts containing all or at least some part of the Greek New Testament. Source: Kurt Aland in *The Journal of Biblical Literature*, vol. 87 (1968), p. 184 summarized in Edward F. Hills, *The King James Version Defended* (Des Moines, Iowa: The Christian Research Press, 1993) p.115.

manuscript having errors of doctrine or which, if accurate, would involve the apostles in historical or other blunders would be seen to be an unreliable witness to the original autographs. However, the practice has been to produce 'eclectic' texts, which reproduce no particular manuscript but construct a text from all available manuscripts making judgements about which reading is best for each word or phrase. At first sight this may seem to be a very worthy project in trying to get the most accurate word but when we realize how many human theories and presuppositions have to be relied upon and that the less *reliable* documents are given the most *influential* place we have to reject both method and findings. The following reasons are apposite.

## *The Subjective has Displaced the Objective*

The need is to seek to increase the certainty as to what is the text of the infallible Scripture and current textual criticism does not do this. Textual transmission should maximize *objectivity* and minimize *subjectivity*. That is, we should not concentrate upon the subjective judgments of men as to what is the infallible scripture but transmit what is available or 'extant'. The primary interest should not be in eclectic texts or subjective choices between variants. The intention should be to increase objectivity but the textual critic must rely to a great extent on his own subjective choices.[3]

## *More* Uncertainty *has been Introduced*

In consequence of the significance of subjective choice with respect to textual criticism there has been no advance in certainty as to the text of Scripture by such criticism but an increase in *uncertainty*. With respect to particular theories of textual criticism the battle cannot be won with excellent academic defences of the *method used*, by reference to history and textual genealogy. Theories in most disciplines have been brilliantly defended only to be proved wrong. Apart from all of the methodological

---

[3] Jakob Van Bruggen explains that the present replacement for the Received Text is 'a consensus-text which has been determined on the basis of *un*certainty. This time no mean from three modern text-*editions*, like the older Nestle, but the mean of the opinions of five modern textual-*critics*. Aland, Black, Martini, Metzger, Wikgren together have established a text by majority-vote.' Jakob Van Bruggen, *The Ancient Text of the New Testament* (Winnipeg: Premier, 1979) p. 10.

debate, a tree is known by its fruits. The question to be asked is, have the present methods of textual criticism based upon a high estimation of a handful of Uncial manuscripts raised to a higher degree our knowledge of what is the original text of Scripture? As a matter of fact it has not achieved what is commonly supposed. The methods have indeed been promoted as having been very successful but the facts speak otherwise. The assessment of the results as a whole must be sought not in the theory but in the New Testament. What then do we find in connection with the variant readings?

The answer is that we find a high degree of *uncertainty* on the part of the textual critics themselves as to what is the true text. Take for example the 150 or so variant readings adopted by the *Revised Version*, 1881, in the Epistle to the Romans. Of these the Anglican Bishop Wordsworth agreed with only 57%. In respect of about one quarter of the variants adopted by the RV, *three or more* textual critics agreed against them. Only in respect of about 25% did Griesbach (1805), Lachmann (1842–1850), Tischendorf (1865–1872), Tregelles (1857–1872), Alford (vol.i. 1868, vol.ii. 1871, vol.iii. 1865, vol.iv. 1862, 1870) and Wordsworth (1870) agree. Thus what some assume to be the assured results of a supposed scientific method are found on closer investigation to be doubtful and disputed opinions.

Almost one hundred years after the *Revised Version* the companion volume to the *United Bible Societies' Greek New Testament* (third edition), *A Textual Commentary on the Greek New Testament* (1975)[4] reveals the same situation. The Preface of the textual commentary states 'One of the chief purposes of the commentary is to set forth the reasons that led the Committee, or a majority of the members of the Committee, to adopt certain variant readings for inclusion in the text and to relegate certain other readings to the apparatus.'[5]

The Introduction explains how, 'In order to indicate the relative degree of certainty in the mind of the Committee for the reading adopted as the text, an identifying letter is included within braces at the beginning of

---

[4] Bruce M. Metzger, *A Textual Commentary on The Greek New Testament* (London: United Bible Societies, 1975)

[5] *Ibid.*, p. v.

116

each set of textual variants. The letter {A} signifies that the text is virtually certain, while {B} indicates that there is some degree of doubt concerning the reading selected for the text. The letter {C} means that there is a considerable degree of doubt whether the text or the apparatus contains the superior reading, while {D} shows that there is a very high degree of doubt concerning the reading selected for the text. In fact, among the {D} decisions sometimes none of the variant readings commended itself as original, and therefore the only recourse was to print the least unsatisfactory reading.'[6]

We should be grateful for this very clear articulation of how the committee felt about the variants that they were incorporating into the now standard New Testament Greek text, as used in Theological colleges, and their further frank statement of their dependence upon *probabilities*. In connection with the latter they state: 'Although the external evidence for two sets of variant readings may be exactly the same, considerations of transcriptional and/or intrinsic probabilities of readings may lead to quite diverse judgments concerning the original text. This is, of course, only another way of saying that textual criticism is an art as well as a science, and demands that each set of variants be evaluated in the light of the fullest consideration of both external evidence and internal probabilities.' In connection with the Gospels the results of their classifications are shown in *Table 10.1*, below.

---

[6] *Ibid.* p. xxviii.

**Degree of Certainty Regarding Readings Chosen in the Gospels**

|  | Unclassified | A | B | C | D |
|---|---|---|---|---|---|
| **Matthew** | 14% | 4% | 32% | 44% | 6% |
| **Mark** | 8% | 21% | 32% | 31% | 8% |
| **Luke** | 14% | 3% | 22% | 49% | 12% |
| **Synoptics** | 12% | 9% | 29% | 41% | 9% |
| **John** | 19% | 12% | 25% | 37% | 7% |
| **Gospels** | 14% | 10% | 28% | 40% | 8% |

*Table 10.1*

**Key:**

A. The text is virtually certain.

B. Some degree of doubt concerning the reading selected for the text.

C. Considerable degree of doubt whether the text or the apparatus correct.

D. A very high degree of doubt concerning the reading selected.

The results shown in the table indicate that there was some degree of doubt expressed in 82% of the variants in Matthew, 71% of the variants in Mark, 83% of the variants in Luke and 69% of those in John. The respective figures for at least 'a considerable degree of doubt' are as follows: Matthew 50%, Mark 39%, Luke 61% and John 44%. The conclusion to which we are drawn is that the current methods of textual criticism do not yield an impressive certainty about the text but on the textual critics' own admission a significant degree of uncertainty.

Readers should appreciate that modern translations merely transmit this *uncertainty*. They are not based upon an existing manuscript but upon an eclectic text where the most that can be said, in connection with the majority of the readings substituted for those of the Received Text, is that they are *'probable'*. If the translator made his own judgement about the variants, then they represent the opinion of that one man as to the correct reading. There may be textual critics who would agree with him, there could be others who would not. In consequence the translated Word of God written becomes a shifting sand, dependent upon the subjective judgements of one or more men. It is a matter of serious concern that this *uncertainty* is transmitted as greater *certainty*. This is especially the case when textual footnotes in modern versions are highly selective and completely fail to draw attention to the uncertainty as to whether the translated reading is correct.

## Major Omissions have Resulted

Doubt is cast on Mark 16.9–20 because these verses are omitted in the Vatican and Sinai manuscripts. This is maintained despite the fact that the verses are found in almost every other manuscript containing Mark's Gospel and in both Irenaeus and Hippolytus who predated the two manuscripts cited. The entire section John 7.53–John 8.11 is considered doubtful or omitted[7] and over a dozen other entire verses of the New Testament are omitted. In total the text of Scripture has been reduced by almost 2%, which is equivalent to the loss of 1st and 2nd Peter.

## The Authority of Scripture has been Impugned

The promise has been that we will be provided with a *more accurate extant text* of Scripture but the end has been that even *the accuracy of the autographs has been denied*! There is, however, a further observation that must be made with respect to the fruits of present methods of textual criticism, which place such an overwhelming value upon the Uncial manuscripts. It should not be forgotten that the use of textual criticism has led in some verses to the introduction into the text of variant readings that imply that the original autographs included a mistake of fact. Clearly we would not expect conservative evangelicals to adopt such readings; but the point being made is that the application of the techniques of textual criticism yields that result.

---

[7] In order to appreciate how subjective the final textual criticism decision becomes see the synopsis of evidence on John 7.53 ff. in William Hendriksen, *The Gospel of John* Volume II (Edinburgh: The Banner of Truth Trust, 1969) pp. 33–35.

Two such examples are found on the first page of the New Testament. In Matthew 1.7–8 *Asaph* is substituted for *Asa* and in Matthew 1.10 *Amos* is substituted for *Amon*. On the former of these the Textual Commentary referred to above comments as follows. 'It is clear that the name "Asaph" is the earliest form of text preserved in the manuscripts, for the agreement of Alexandrian (Aleph and B) and Caesarean witnesses (f¹ f¹³ 700 1071) with Eastern versions (cop arm eth geo) and representatives of the Western text (Old Latin mss. and D in Luke [D is lacking for this part of Matthew]) makes a very strong combination. Furthermore, the tendency of scribes, observing that the name of the psalmist Asaph (cf. the titles of Ps 50 and 73 to 83) was confused with that of Asa the king of Judah (1 Kgs 15.9ff.), would have been to correct the error, thus accounting for the prevalence of Ἀσά in the later Ecclesiastical text and its inclusion in the Textus Receptus.'[8]

As we have said, we are not suggesting that conservative evangelical scholars are prepared to make such substitutions. Indeed it is precisely because they are not prepared to do so that the argument against the present presuppositions and methods of textual criticism is strengthened. If they consistently applied the rules they use elsewhere with variants they would, at a minimum, have to include (in a footnote) *Asaph* and *Amos* as alternative readings found in some of the 'best' manuscripts. I use the term 'best' in this connection according to the evaluation of these manuscripts by translators of modern versions.

Of course you will look in vain for such footnotes in the *New International Version* or some conservative evangelical commentaries; and it is not surprising that conservative evangelicals are accused by some of applying double standards, following the 'scientific' methods of contemporary textual criticism until it cuts across the presupposition of an inspired scripture, when it is replaced by dogmatic considerations.

More openness by conservative evangelical scholars on such points would be refreshing. Some statement as to where the textual evidence points 'on current theories' followed by the reasons for its rejection would at least prepare Christian folk so that they are not utterly confused

---

[8] Bruce M. Metzger, *op. cit.*, p. 1.

when someone draws out a modern edition of the Greek New Testament and shows them that the Uncial manuscripts so highly regarded by conservative evangelical translators read 'Asaph' and 'Amos'. It is not enough to hide behind some scholarly mystic so that faith ultimately comes to rest upon the wisdom of men, even godly men. The flock is to have direct access to the Scripture and the wisdom of God. The present importation of uncertainty about what is Scripture will unsettle faith, transfer it to an existential 'leap in the dark' or blinkered 'head in the sand' approach which says, 'I don't understand the issues but I will go on believing notwithstanding.' Far to be preferred is that the people are given the full facts about the fruits of textual criticism pursued on the basis of present assumptions. They can then judge for themselves the value of methods that lead to the conclusion that the inspired Matthew was *mistaken*. Thus, when all the academic eloquence is expended, the faithful follower of Christ will have more reserve about the presuppositions of a textual criticism that yields such fruit.

## *The Quality of Some Manuscripts has been Overstated*

The Reformed tradition has had solid scholarly commentators who have shown themselves much more reserved about the 'assured' results of textual criticism than the textual critics themselves and some contemporary evangelical translators. Reference can be made, for example, to J. A. Alexander. In Acts 2.47 the *New International Version* follows the textual critics in omitting the word 'church.' On Acts 5.11 Alexander comments 'This is the second instance of the use of this word in the book before us, or the first, according to some ancient manuscripts and recent critics, who omit the word (ἐκκλησία) in 2,47.'[9] In Acts 8 the *New International Version* relegates verse 37 to a footnote merely stating: 'Some late manuscripts' and then adding the verse. Alexander has a detailed note as follows: 'This verse is excluded from the text by the latest critics, because wanting in several of the oldest manuscripts and versions, while in many copies which contain it, there is a diversity of form, both in the words themselves and in their order, which is commonly considered a suspicious circumstance. The interpolation is

---

[9] J. A. Alexander, *A Commentary on the Acts of the Apostles* (Edinburgh: The Banner of Truth Trust, 1984) p. 201.

accounted for, as an attempt to guard against the practice of precipitate admission to the church, in favour of which this verse might with some plausibility have been alleged. But on the other hand, it may be argued that the verse, though genuine, was afterwards omitted, as unfriendly to the practice of delaying baptism, which had become common, if not prevalent, before the end of the third century. It is moreover found in many manuscripts, including some of the most ancient, and is quoted as a part of this context, not only by Cyprian but by Irenaeus. It is therefore one of those cases, in which the external testimony may be looked upon as very nearly balanced, and in which it is the safest course to let the scale of the received text and traditional belief preponderate.'[10] Our purpose here is not to enter into an extended treatment of particular variants but merely to illustrate how Alexander states the facts so that the reader is aware of the issues. Although Alexander accepted textual criticism, he by no means manifests the enthusiasm of our modern translators for all of the assumptions of the textual critics. Without overstating the case it can be said that once '*ancient* manuscripts' is replaced by '*best* manuscripts' a much less cautious approach appears to prevail. It can only be said that if 'Asaph' does not spell caution with respect to Uncial priority it is hard to see what will.

*Fundamental Error has been Surreptitiously Introduced into the Scriptures*

The text critic's method has led directly to the denial of the infallibility of the *autographs* written by the inspired men. These writings, according to the findings of the textual critics, were *not* free from error. Let us for a moment consider the effect in an evangelical congregation where a preacher turns up who uses a translation of one of the earliest Alexandrian manuscripts available. He begins to read in Matthew and chapter one. At verse seven he reads, 'and Abia begat Asaph' and in verse eight he reads, 'and Asaph begat Josaphat.' At verse ten he reads, 'and Manasses begat Amos; and Amos begat Josias.' Let us assume that there are those in the congregation sufficiently instructed in the Old Testament to recognize the mistakes, which if authentic, would have involved Matthew in two historical blunders. Now suppose they object to

---

[10] *Ibid.*, pp. 349–350.

the preacher and he replies that he is using one of the *very best* manuscripts available. It seems to me that the listening believers would be unlikely to be persuaded, having their own ears as witnesses that either they must accept that an infallible Scripture is a delusion, or that some very ancient scribe producing one of the *very best* manuscripts could make such blunders. If he could make such blunders how many less obvious mistakes might he have made? If this is one of the very best manuscripts what sort of access can we expect to have to the original text when such blatant corruptions are in the best? If the visiting preacher is to be believed the congregation must sacrifice the infallibility of the Bible and belief in a reliable transmission of the text of Scripture. Alternatively, the early Alexandrian manuscript can be put back into cold storage where instructed hearers would always have left it.

There is, however, a more subtle way of introducing the Alexandrian textual tradition. The manuscripts are embodied into a scholastic theory of textual transmission and are accorded the role of revising the common textual tradition. In evangelical circles, however, certain of the facts have to be kept in the background and value judgements are put in their place. Consider the effects on the distribution and use of the *New International Version*, for example, if at Matthew 1.7–8 a footnote had been inserted reading, 'The two most reliable early manuscripts, which do not have Mark 16.9–20, read *Amos*.' There would doubtless have been many Christians who would have decided that they had different perceptions of the reliability of the said documents. They might have legitimately concluded that to describe the Alexandrian manuscripts as 'ancient' is well founded but to describe them as 'the most reliable', as the *New International Version* does, is *impossible*. History demonstrates that scholars get enthusiastic about theories. The hearing faithful should not.

## *Questionable Scholarship has been Employed*

In a recent work on early Syriac translation technique[11], P. J. Williams has drawn attention to the invalid assumption that whenever an ancient translation differed from the original Hebrew or Greek a lost reading accounted for the variation. Williams shows by reference to the Syriac

---

[11] P. J. Williams, *Early Syriac Translation Technique and the Textual Criticism of the Greek Gospels* (Gorgias Press, 2004).

that the scholars in fact *create* the variants by assuming the translations to be of a literal kind. These variants then become a basis for altering the Hebrew or Greek text of Scripture.

## The Need to Return to Objectivity

The providence of God has shut up the conservative evangelical tradition to one course of action if it would faithfully transmit the text of Scripture as opposed to the opinions of men. It must transmit and translate that textual tradition which we know to have been in use in the Church. It must publish contemporary *opinions* about the state of that text in a separate volume. The introduction of variants into the text at this stage of history can only add confusion as to what is Scripture in the minds of the people. There are many non-evangelicals who desire just that result. Unlike the Saviour they have no confidence in Scripture authority themselves and desire others to be similarly 'free' to judge the Word of God instead of being judged by it. Our task is firstly, to faithfully transmit what God has given to us in His providence – the common ecclesiastical text; and, secondly, to give balanced judgements about variations from that text. In this way the objective Word is separated from contemporary subjective opinion. Only when these two roles are separated will the erosion of confidence as to what is Scripture be reversed. In point of fact the received text backed by the Byzantine tradition is the only text around which the people of God can unite, because, as amendments are introduced into eclectic texts on the basis of *probability*, the less support those texts will command from those who have different presuppositions about the methods of textual criticism or who come to different conclusions when using the same method. The prerequisite for the battle of faith is a common Bible and this is secured by transmitting in translation what God has given to us in his providence and doing this separately from our subjective judgements about textual variants.

## TRANSLATIONS

The position of the Westminster Confession is that, from the extant Hebrew and Greek originals, translations into the common tongue are to be made. These are to be accomplished with reverential care. Nothing is stated in the confessions about the quality of translations. Experience shows that they do in fact vary greatly in quality, from the very good, through the mediocre, to the very bad. It is therefore of supreme importance to have accurate translations of the providentially preserved text of Scripture. Accurate translations of the Bible are still authoritative, infallible and error-free *Scripture*. The Apostles quoted the Septuagint translation of the Old Testament *as Scripture* in their writings. However, the subjective element is greater in a translation than in a copy of the original Hebrew or Greek because choices have to be made concerning appropriate equivalent words to translate the original. In translation, the *Word of God* must be expressed in the *words of men*. The final appeal must consequently be made to the original languages. An accurate translation based upon a reliable copy may, however, be more reliable than an eclectic Hebrew or Greek text if the presuppositions upon which the eclectic text is based are unreliable and lead to many significant departures from the authentic scripture. Translation from an accurate copy does not require textual criticism in order to produce a reliable version though the usefulness of the latter could be increased by a supplement indicating significant variants in reliable manuscripts. A translator may thus be a good translator without competence in textual criticism and produce a usable translation. With respect to translation of the scriptures a distinction may be made between existing translations and new translations and with respect to the latter a distinction can be made between completely new translations and the revision of existing translations.

With respect to the republication of *existing* translations, this is a matter of *transmission*. The task can be completely objective if the translation is reproduced as it stands. This is faithful to the original translators and it is the way in which scholarly reproduction is done; the effort is made to reproduce an original according to what it is. It is a legitimate activity to transmit a *reliable* translation of the scriptures even though it is not *perfect*. Explanatory notes can be added by way of a supplement, in the interests of explaining problems of text or translation in the version. In this way subjective judgments about preferred readings or translations are separated from the objective reproduction. By adopting a particular translation we do not state that it is the *only* reliable translation; but by rejecting a particular translation we do state that *that* translation is unacceptable. Decisions about which translation(s) to republish should be related to the quality of the translation. A literal word for word translation is seldom readable. A 'dynamic equivalence' translation reproduces the thoughts of the original document without attention to the grammatical form of the original and loses considerable accuracy. Between these two extremes is the 'formal equivalence' translation, which seeks, as far as possible, to follow the grammar and wording of the original.[12] This latter kind of translation is faithful to the principle that inspiration resulted not only in the communication of ideas but involved those ideas being communicated in *particular* words. 'Which things also we speak, not *in the words* which man's wisdom teacheth, but *which the Holy Ghost teacheth*; comparing spiritual things with spiritual.'[13] It is, therefore, important to seek to use the equivalent English words, as far as possible, in translation. In this way maximum accuracy is preserved.

A *new translation* is a much more ambitious undertaking than a revision and the 'formal equivalence' translation standard should be applied. Translation involves a level of subjective choice and the highest standard is attained when a person or persons of outstanding theological and linguistic competence work from reliable copies of the Hebrew Old Testament and the Greek New Testament. Important textual variants within the tradition and alternative translations could be embodied in a supplement. Where this standard is not attainable it may still be possible to provide key portions of the scriptures in a particular foreign language. It is only in the providence of God that men of sufficient competence are raised up to translate the scriptures into particular languages. Normally the competence level described above for new translations would be

---

[12] Robert Martin distinguishes these latter two methods as follows: 'The dynamic equivalence translation is based on the principle of "equivalent effect" rather than on the principle of "formal linguistic equivalence."' By "equivalent effect" is meant that the translator tries to discern what the "impact" of the original would have been on the original readers and then he tries to use the English style and idiom which will make a similar... impact on the modern reader.' 'The formal equivalence... method of translating attempts to say "what" the original text says by retaining "how" it says it (as far as English grammar allows). Although clear English expression does not always allow the formal equivalence translator to do so, he tries not to adjust the idioms which the original writer used; rather, he attempts to render them more or less literally, so that the reader may be able to perceive something of the way in which the original document employed local linguistic and cultural elements to convey ideas.' Robert P. Martin, *Accuracy of Translation: The Primary Criterion in Evaluating Bible Versions with special reference to the New International Version* (Edinburgh: The Banner of Truth Trust, 1997) p. 8.

[13] 1 Corinthians 2.13.

found among pastors and teachers or such of them as have devoted their time to theological training. The value of producing lower quality translations of the whole Bible is questionable when scripture portions in the designated language can meet the need for scripture until a high quality translation of the Bible can be completed.

The *revision of an existing translation* arises where it is the practical way to attain to a translation in a particular language when resources would not permit a full new translation or where it is desired to maintain the gains of the translation to be revised. It provides an opportunity to improve the accuracy of the translation. The finished revision should manifest the 'formal equivalence' standard of translation. Often revisions have been used to alter the character of the version revised. The *Revised Version* as republished in 1959 claims to be *the Holy Bible containing the Old and New Testaments translated out of the original tongues: being the version set forth AD 1611 compared with the most ancient authorities and revised.* In fact it introduced into the Authorized Version 1611 tradition alien textual views based upon dubious subjective opinions about many readings in the originals. Martin draws attention to the fact that the *Revised Standard Version* set out to revise the *American Standard Version.* The latter was based upon 'formal equivalence' principles but the revisers were not committed to this principle. According to Martin the revisers ended up producing a 'philosophically schizophrenic' document.[14] With respect to the accuracy of translations and their revisions, it is necessary to ask the following questions:

1. Is the translation based upon reliable Hebrew and Greek manuscripts?

2. Has any textual criticism employed been based upon sound principles?

3. Did the translators employ the 'formal equivalence' standard of translation?

4. Did the translators maintain that reverence for the Bible that it ought to have as the Word of God?

---

[14] Robert P. Martin, *op. cit.,* p. 10.

## INTERPRETATION

Interpretation of scripture passages or the whole Bible is embodied in commentaries. Because of the link between context, variants, meaning and translation, commenting upon the text of scripture includes judgments concerning variants within the reliable copies of the scripture, the correct text, the correct translation and the meaning of the text. Reformed commentators make different judgments about these matters. The interpretation and application of scripture is committed to those men described in the scripture as pastors and teachers who are called and gifted for the task. It is not the place of Bible Societies to intrude upon the work of the ministry but they can facilitate that work by placing copies of the reliable extant Hebrew and Greek texts in the hands of ministers and by placing reliable translations of the Word of God in the hands of the people of God. A Bible Society should seek as far as possible to transmit a reliable original text and reliable translations. Judgments with respect to variants and alternative translations should be kept to a minimum consistent with completing these tasks to a high standard of accuracy following the advice of Reformed ministers.

Variants and alternative translations must, to some extent, be considered in the commentaries. Scholars, however, should refrain from foisting onto the people of God a host of human judgements based upon fallible opinions. These can only fragment the Church in its common cause, if given some pretended authority beyond what the evidence can sustain. As we have shown textual criticism as a basis for textual transmission and translation merely increases uncertainty, leaving believers bewildered by variations whose status, according to the critics themselves, does not go beyond the probable. The scholar Edward F. Hills provides a conservative approach to textual criticism in his book *The King James Version Defended* first published in 1956. It should be read by anyone who has a serious interest in the scriptural approach to textual transmission.[15]

---

[15] Edward F. Hills, *The King James Version Defended* (Des Moines, Iowa: The Christian Research Press, 1984)

# Chapter 11

## *The Supremacy Of The Self-Interpreting Scripture*

*Acts 28.17–29*

'And it came to pass, that after three days Paul called the chief of the Jews together: and when they were come together, he said unto them, Men and brethren, though I have committed nothing against the people, or customs of our fathers, yet was I delivered prisoner from Jerusalem into the hands of the Romans. Who, when they had examined me, would have let me go, because there was no cause of death in me. But when the Jews spake against it, I was constrained to appeal unto Caesar; not that I had ought to accuse my nation of. For this cause therefore have I called for you, to see you, and to speak with you: because that for the hope of Israel I am bound with this chain. And they said unto him, We neither received letters out of Judaea concerning thee, neither any of the brethren that came shewed or spake any harm of thee. But we desire to hear of thee what thou thinkest: for as concerning this sect, we know that every where it is spoken against. And when they had appointed him a day, there came many to him into his lodging; to whom he expounded and testified the kingdom of God, persuading them concerning Jesus, both out of the law of Moses, and out of the prophets, from morning till evening. And some believed the things which were spoken, and some believed not. And when they agreed not among themselves, they departed, after that Paul had spoken one word, Well spake the Holy Ghost by Esaias the prophet unto our fathers, Saying, Go unto this people, and say, Hearing ye shall hear, and shall not understand; and seeing ye shall see, and not perceive: For the heart of this people is waxed gross, and their ears are dull of hearing, and their eyes have they closed; lest they should see with their eyes, and hear with their ears, and understand with their heart, and should be converted, and I should heal them. Be it known therefore unto you, that the salvation of God is sent unto the Gentiles, and that they will hear it. And when he had said these words, the Jews departed, and had great reasoning among themselves.'

The background to these verses is Paul's desire to make it clear to the Jews at Rome that he had not sought in any way to incite hatred of the Jews (verses 17–20). Christianity is at its core a message of love. God has manifested his love to the world: 'For God so loved the world, that he gave his only begotten Son, that whosoever believeth in him should not perish, but have everlasting life.'[1] In all their labours Christians are impelled by love: 'For whether we be beside ourselves, it is to God: or whether we be sober, it is for your cause. For the love of Christ constraineth us...'[2] Paul was not motivated by hatred of his own people but intense desire for their salvation: 'Brethren, my heart's desire and prayer to God for Israel is, that they might be saved.'[3] God's love to us impels us to love others and desire their good. The highest good we can do for others is to share with them the Gospel. This, however, can give rise to contention: 'some believed the things which were spoken, and some believed not' (verse 24). Who is to decide who is right? Only God speaking in his written word is entitled so to do. We must consider: (1) the *supremacy* of the Scripture, (2) the *self-interpreting* character of Scripture and (3) the *Spirit of God speaking* in Scripture.

## The *Supremacy* of Scripture

The supremacy of Scripture was the presupposition behind the apostolic method. The Jews said: 'But we desire to hear of thee what thou thinkest: for as concerning this sect, we know that every where it is spoken against' (verse 22). Consequently 'when they had appointed him a day, there came many to him into his lodging; to whom *he expounded and testified the kingdom of God*, persuading them concerning Jesus, both *out*

---

[1] John 3.16.
[2] 2 Corinthians 5.13–14.
[3] Romans 10.1.

*of the law of Moses, and out of the prophets,* from morning till evening' (verse 23). What Paul *thought* was what the scriptures *taught.* He had learned submission to the Word concerning Christ: 'For though we walk in the flesh, we do not war after the flesh: (For the weapons of our warfare are not carnal, but mighty through God to the pulling down of strong holds;) Casting down imaginations, and every high thing that exalteth itself against the knowledge of God, and bringing into captivity every thought to the obedience of Christ...'[4] Many Christians find such a thing hard because they want to be the master of their own vessel and dictate their own movements. Such an attitude makes for weakness, promoting division, erroneous teaching and lack of growth as Paul found and had to deal with among the Corinthians: 'Now I beseech you, brethren, by the name of our Lord Jesus Christ, that ye all speak the same thing, and that there be no divisions among you; but that ye be perfectly joined together in the same mind and in the same judgment. For it hath been declared unto me of you, my brethren, by them which are of the house of Chloe, that there are contentions among you.'[5] Again he writes: 'And I, brethren, could not speak unto you as unto spiritual, but as unto carnal, even as unto babes in Christ. I have fed you with milk, and not with meat: for hitherto ye were not able to bear it, neither yet now are ye able. For ye are yet carnal: for whereas there is among you envying, and strife, and divisions, are ye not carnal, and walk as men?'[6] So he explains that there is but one foundation and that all must build consistently with the word of Christ: 'According to the grace of God which is given unto me, as a wise masterbuilder, I have laid the foundation, and another buildeth thereon. But let every man take heed how he buildeth thereupon. For other foundation can no man lay than that is laid, which is Jesus Christ. Now if any man build upon this foundation gold, silver, precious stones, wood, hay, stubble; Every man's work shall be made manifest: for the day shall declare it, because it shall be revealed by fire; and the fire shall try every man's work of what sort it is.'[7]

---

[4] 2 Corinthians 10.3–5.

[5] 1 Corinthians 1.10–11.

[6] 1 Corinthians 3.1–3.

[7] 1 Corinthians 3.10–13.

The Apostle would have the Jews persuaded but only out of the scriptures. His method was exposition: 'he *expounded* and testified the kingdom of God, persuading them concerning Jesus, both *out of the law of Moses*, and *out of the prophets*...' He shunned the Jewish tradition that he knew so well and had no time for the philosophy of this world or its eloquence. He was not out to win arguments, impress others with his own personality or display his learning. He simply expounds what is in the Word of God. *It* must decide any matters of difference. As Philip Henry explains: 'Conversion turns us to the Word of God, as our touchstone, to examine ourselves... as our glass, to dress by (James 1); as our rule to walk and work by (Galatians 6.16); as our water to wash us (Psalm 119.9); as our fire to warm us (Luke 24); as our food to nourish us (Job 23.12); as our sword to fight with (Ephesians 6); as our counsellor, in all our doubts (Psalm 119.24); as our cordial, to comfort us; as our heritage, to enrich us.'[8] So the Confession extols the supremacy of the Scripture: 'The supreme judge by which all controversies of religion are to be determined, and all decrees of councils, opinions of ancient writers, doctrines of men, and private spirits, are to be examined; and in whose sentence we are to rest; can be no other but the Holy Spirit speaking in the Scripture.'[9] This was the Apostles' way. The teaching of Scripture was always the decisive thing: 'But there rose up certain of the sect of the Pharisees which believed, saying, That it was needful to circumcise them, and to command them to keep the law of Moses. *And the apostles and elders came together for to consider of this matter.* And when there had been much disputing, Peter rose up, and said unto them, Men and brethren, ye know how that a good while ago God made choice among us, that the Gentiles by my mouth should hear the word of the gospel, and believe. And God, which knoweth the hearts, bare them witness, giving them the Holy Ghost, even as he did unto us; And put no difference between us and them, purifying

---

[8] Quoted in I. D. E. Thomas, *The Golden Treasury of Puritan Quotations* (Edinburgh: The Banner of Truth Trust, 1997) p.33.

[9] 'The Confession of Faith of the Westminster Assembly of Divines' Chapter 1.10 in S. W. Carruthers (ed.), *The Westminster Confession of Faith* (Manchester: R. Aikman & Son, 1937) p. 93.

their hearts by faith. Now therefore why tempt ye God, to put a yoke upon the neck of the disciples, which neither our fathers nor we were able to bear? But we believe that through the grace of the Lord Jesus Christ we shall be saved, even as they. Then all the multitude kept silence, and gave audience to Barnabas and Paul, declaring what miracles and wonders God had wrought among the Gentiles by them. And after they had held their peace, James answered, saying, Men and brethren, hearken unto me: Simeon hath declared how God at the first did visit the Gentiles, to take out of them a people for his name. *And to this agree the words of the prophets; as it is written,* After this I will return, and will build again the tabernacle of David, which is fallen down; and I will build again the ruins thereof, and I will set it up: That the residue of men might seek after the Lord, and all the Gentiles, upon whom my name is called, saith the Lord, who doeth all these things. Known unto God are all his works from the beginning of the world. Wherefore my sentence is, that we trouble not them, which from among the Gentiles are turned to God.'[10]

## The *Self-interpreting* Character of Scripture

There is a problem that arises when we look at scripture as supreme. The questions arise: Do not the Jehovah's Witnesses and other sects use the scriptures? Do not the Mormons and others too? Does not each have his own interpretation of different passages? Who then is to be taken as having the correct interpretation? There are several considerations to bear in mind.

### We must use the whole Scripture

The Apostle was 'persuading them concerning Jesus, both *out of the law of Moses,* and *out of the prophets.*' These were well known divisions of the Word of God. We have the fuller common expression at the mouth of the Lord Jesus: 'These are the words which I spake unto you, while I was yet with you, that all things must be fulfilled, which were written in *the law of Moses,* and in *the prophets,* and in *the psalms,* concerning me. Then opened he their understanding, that they might understand *the*

---

[10] Acts 15.5–19.

*scriptures.*'[11] The use of the *whole* Scripture was our Lord's method. A text here and a text there taken out of context can be made to mean most things that anyone would have it to mean. So we might take what Paul writes to Timothy: 'For there is one God, and one mediator between God and men, the man Christ Jesus'[12] and from this conclude that Jesus was truly man, which is accurate. If we drew the conclusion that he was no more than a man it would be false because elsewhere we read: 'And the *Word* was made flesh, and dwelt among us, (and we beheld his glory, the glory as of the *only begotten of the Father*,) full of grace and truth.'[13] Thus we must follow Christ's example and Paul's example and use the whole of the Scripture.

## We must let Scripture interpret Scripture

Religion is in a bad state today because people want a *potted* version of everything. We are used to fast food, instant-access savings, central locking, the quick fix, sound-bites and so on but the Bible is not a course of tablets to be taken one by one. The Bible is a tapestry to be examined with care as the Westminster Confession explains: 'The infallible rule of interpretation of Scripture is the Scripture itself: and therefore, when there is a question about the true and full sense of any Scripture (which is not manifold, but one), it must be searched and known by other places that speak more clearly.'[14]

## The Principle of interpretation is 'Mutual Exposition'

When the whole of the Scripture is used we find that Moses explains the Prophets and the Prophets explain Moses. The Old Testament explains the New Testament and the New Testament sheds light on the Old. The sense of Scripture is *one* and therefore one part must not be interpreted to contradict another part. If four pieces of a jigsaw puzzle fit perfectly

---

[11] Luke 24.44–45.

[12] 1 Timothy 2.5.

[13] John 1.14.

[14] 'The Confession of Faith of the Westminster Assembly of Divines' Chapter 1.9 in S. W. Carruthers (ed.), *The Westminster Confession of Faith* (Manchester: R. Aikman & Son, 1937) p. 92.

together around a space it is no good dislodging two of them to force an alien piece into the space. In the same way we must not force our alien interpretations into one passage against the clear teaching of other passages. *Each* must be consistent with *all* and in this way the Scripture controls our interpretations and not vice versa.

## The Spirit of God Speaking in Scripture

The times have not changed. As it is now so it was then: 'some believed the things which were spoken, and some believed not' (verse 24). Many want to evade the force of Gospel preaching. It does not fit their life-style. They do not want the sovereignty of God for example. They deny the total depravity of man and want to maintain something left in man that will take the initiative in responding to God. They cannot tolerate God's unconditional election because that leaves the choice with God and not with man. They do not like the doctrine of limited atonement, which emphasizes that redemption was particular and that Christ loved the Church and gave himself for *it*. They cannot accept God's irresistible grace and that Christ's people will be made willing in the day of his power not by *forcing* their wills but by *transforming* them. They care nothing for final perseverance because it is viewed as removing the incentive to continue in the grace of God whereas it gives us the incentive to make our calling and election sure. However, if a doctrine is scriptural then resistance to it is resistance to God. As we saw above 'the supreme judge' is 'the Holy Spirit speaking in the Scripture.' It is the voice not of man but of God. The scorn of sinners is hurtful to the godly preacher, not on account of his own reputation, but because he sees that it dishonours God with terrible consequence to the impenitent scoffer. Hence the reaction of the Apostle: 'And when they agreed not among themselves, they departed, after that Paul had spoken one word, Well spake the Holy Ghost by Esaias the prophet unto our fathers, Saying, Go unto this people, and say, Hearing ye shall hear, and shall not understand; and seeing ye shall see, and not perceive: For the heart of this people is waxed gross, and their ears are dull of hearing, and their eyes have they closed; lest they should see with their eyes, and hear with their ears, and understand with their heart, and should be converted, and

I should heal them.'[15] How personal the reproofs of the Word of God are! Paul says that Isaiah spoke 'unto *our fathers.*' The Spirit speaks to real people through the human authors of the Bible. He is speaking to you and to me today. It is so individual. You cannot afford not to listen. So we read in Hebrews: 'Wherefore (*as the Holy Ghost saith,* To day *if ye will hear* his voice, Harden not your hearts, as in the provocation, in the day of temptation in the wilderness: When your fathers tempted me, proved me, and saw my works forty years. Wherefore I was grieved with that generation, and said, They do alway err in their heart; and they have not known my ways. So I sware in my wrath, They shall not enter into my rest.) Take heed, brethren, lest there be *in any of you* an evil heart of unbelief, in departing from the living God. But exhort one another daily, while it is called To day; *lest any of you* be hardened through the deceitfulness of sin. For we are made partakers of Christ, if we hold the beginning of our confidence stedfast unto the end.'[16]

---

[15] Acts 28.25–27.
[16] Hebrews 3.7–14.

# Chapter 12

## *The Applications Of Scripture: Ministry, Ethics And Apologetics*

The authority of Scripture necessitates that the doctrines learned from it are to be applied in the various departments of our thinking and practice. In this chapter we will relate what we have learned thus far about the scriptures and their supreme authority to pastoral and ecclesiastical practice, morality and ethics and apologetics. In Chapter 13 Theological training will be addressed.

### Pastoral and Ecclesiastical

#### *Church Government*

God has given a supernatural saving revelation of himself and his will to his Church. Formerly it was given part by part in different ways. Latterly a completed revelation has been given through Christ and the whole finally committed to writing. With the cessation of visions, dreams, audible voices and so on, the word of God written has become the only source of authority for the regulation of the Church. As the rule of faith and practice it is unique, complete, clear and final.

#### *Evangelism*

The scriptural evidence considered in previous chapters makes the situation with respect to evangelism very clear. It is not the task of evangelism to prove that a personal Creator exists. The evidence is being daily presented that there is a Creator, independent of his creation who is eternal, infinitely wise, almighty, good and righteous. These invisible things of God are understood from his creation. God is known as the personal Creator, Architect, Benefactor, Preserver, Governor, Legislator and Judge. The Church goes out into the world to those who are inexcusable for their denial of the truth and suppression and distortion of the facts, but it does so with a message of hope. Although general revelation makes no discovery of the way of salvation, God's special revelation does, and the proclamation of this message is absolutely necessary to salvation. The inexcusability of sinners and the insufficiency of general revelation add urgency to the evangelistic task at home and abroad. No amount of reasoning on the basis of the revelation of God the Creator will lead a condemned sinner to an understanding of the way of salvation. The materials for such an understanding are not to be found by a consideration of the light of nature or the works of creation and providence. We may not adopt a complacent attitude like Deism which maintained that such consideration would be sufficient to provide a knowledge of God's being and will produce eternal happiness. Sinners need to know about God's gracious provision of forgiveness in Christ and it is only in the scriptures that this is now revealed. 'For whosoever shall call upon the name of the Lord shall be saved. How then shall they call on him in whom they have not believed? and how shall they believe in him of whom they have not heard? and how shall they hear without a preacher? ...So then faith cometh by hearing, and hearing by the word of God.'[1] The Church is not to entangle itself in worldly wisdom or methods. The content of its message is scripturally defined, it is *the preaching of the cross;*[2] and the method of communication is scripturally defined, it is *by the foolishness of preaching, ...not with excellency of speech or of wisdom.*[3] Ministers of the Gospel are not philosophers, commentators, entertainers or salesmen. They spearhead the witness of the Church to the world by expounding God's word written. Only so can they be faithful to the apostolic message and method.

## Worship

*Prayer.* Prayer cannot be attained by the dictates of nature. Scripture reveals the only mediator through whom sinners can approach to God. Intellectual attainments by heathen philosophers in natural or moral philosophy could not teach them how to call upon the name of the covenant God. Consequently Paul could not approve their devotions but declared 'Whom therefore ye ignorantly worship, him declare I unto you.

---

[1] Romans 10.13–14,17.

[2] 1 Corinthians 1.18.

[3] 1 Corinthians 1.21, 2.1.

God that made the world and all things therein...'[4] preaching to them their need to repent of their ways. [5]

*Preaching.* General revelation has relevance to the preaching of the gospel. Shaw identifies the following purposes of the knowledge of God the Creator and Lawgiver:

> It witnesses to God's goodness.
>
> It shows us our duty.
>
> It convinces us of sin.
>
> It restrains from extreme wickedness.
>
> It excites to seek a clearer revelation of God.
>
> It prepares men to receive the Gospel.
>
> It vindicates God's actions as Judge.[6]

Such revelation does not require us to seek to formulate rational proofs for the existence of God. The insufficiency of general revelation does not lie in an inability to convince sinners of the existence, power, wisdom, goodness and justice of God; but in the fact that it does not make known how sinners can be saved. By the light of nature people can recognise evil in the world but they cannot find the remedy to guilt, corruption and judgement. For sinners the problem with general revelation is not that it is unclear but that it is too clear. To evade its force requires suppression of the facts. Our task is not to prove that God exists but to expound from his special revelation the way of salvation including why sinful man's reaction to general revelation is what it is.

---

[4] Acts 17.23b–24a.

[5] Acts 17.30.

[6] Robert Shaw, *The Reformed Faith: An Exposition of the Confession of Faith of the Westminster Assembly of Divines* (Inverness: Christian Focus Publications, 1973) p. 4.

*Praise.* The nineteenth Psalm opens *'the books of God'*: the *'book of creation and providence'* and the *'book of inspiration'*.

> *'The heav'ns God's glory do declare,*
> *the skies his hand-works preach:*
> *Day utters speech to day, and night*
> *to night doth knowledge teach.*
> There is no speech nor tongue to which
> their voice doth not extend:
> Their line is gone through all the earth,
> their words to the world's end.

> 'In them he set the sun a tent;
> Who, bridegroom-like, forth goes
> From's chamber, as a strong man doth
> to run his race rejoice.
> From heav'n's end is his going forth,
> circling to th' end again;
> And there is nothing from his heat
> that hidden doth remain.

> *'God's law is perfect, and converts*
> *the soul in sin that lies:*
> *God's testimony is most sure,*
> *and makes the simple wise.*
> The statutes of the Lord are right,
> and do rejoice the heart:
> The Lord's command is pure, and doth
> light to the eyes impart.'[7]

## Morality and Ethics

*Morality*

Without Christianity and the Bible people understand that they are moral beings. This is the natural condition of us all. Even the worst of sinners are not amoral animals and perfectly sane people can be extremely

---

[7] Psalm 19.1–8, *The Psalms of David in Metre: According to the Version Approved by the Church of Scotland, and Appointed to be Used in Worship.*

wicked. The heathen idolaters with all of their vile affections, fornication, covetousness and murder knew the judgement of God against their sins.[8] Though fallen and without God's special revelation in his written word they had a moral consciousness. Our study to this point enables us to state the following propositions concerning Paul's ethical teaching.

1. We all have a knowledge of right and wrong arising from the demands of the Divine law inscribed within us: the work of the law written in our hearts. God's law is so embedded in us that we cannot escape from it.

2. We have a conscience which, without reference to the law of Moses, can refer to the work of the law written in our hearts approving what is good and accusing us concerning our wrong doing.

3. We show by our behaviour that we have knowledge of what God's law requires and that this knowledge exerts an influence upon our conduct. However corrupted, this natural instinct to do the things contained in the law cannot be completely eradicated.

4. We have an awareness of the judgement of God and know that the wages of sin is death.[9] However we may go against it, Paul states that we know the judgement of God, that they which commit such things are worthy of death.

5. These are all relevant to mature sane humanity.[10]

## Modernist Rationality

The morality described in the previous paragraph is Theistic. It is based upon the existence of God (Greek θεός, *theos*, hence 'Theism'). Theism accepts that the Divine Lawgiver prescribes what is good and what is evil according to his own character, which is holy and righteous. The atheist

---

[8] Romans 1.21–32.

[9] Romans 6.23.

[10] See Romans 2.14–15.

(a-theist, 'not theistic') denies the existence of such a personal God and must rely upon human reason to arrive at a basis for life. The judgement of scripture on atheism is uncompromising: 'The fool hath said in his heart, There is no God.'[11] The atheist's own conscience and daily observations witness against his denial. As we have seen in the previous section, conscience is not on the side of Atheism but of Theism. Its witness is that there is a God, that God is a Lawgiver, that the work of his law is written in our hearts and that by reference to it our conscience can approve what is good and condemn what is evil.

Philosophical attempts to frame an alternative system of ethics without reference to the God of revelation require the identification and application of a moral principle or principles that can be applied to determine what is a good action or the good life. Reference might be made to virtues, pleasure, happiness, motive, obligation and so on. No particular approach has commanded universal support and moral consensus has been lost. The moral consensus of the Middle Ages, based upon Aristotle, gave way under the pressures of the Renaissance and Enlightenment. This led to a new scientific criterion that rejected ecclesiastical authority and sought validation on the basis of empirical investigations. Kant's response was to locate authority in the rational individual but to require that whatever moral laws the individual decided upon, that same individual should be prepared to accept that everyone would have to keep them. This provided for a rational source of authority and universality. Other approaches chose other starting points within the modernist rationality resulting in dissensus. This provided the opportunity for Positivism to confine rational investigation to statements that could be verified by empirical investigations. Moral statements were reduced to no more than moral opinions leading to ethical relativism.

That this has now worked its way through into the schooling of children is evident. Dr Nick Tate, the Government's chief curriculum adviser at the time, warned of the 'dragon of relativism' that must be slain. Post-modernism has drawn attention to the Positivist rationality as reductionist and restrictive and seeks either to secure integration through dialogue; or, accepting the cultural and moral diversity, seeks to utilise it

---

[11] Psalm 14.1.

for moral development through rational dialogue. One cannot deny the impressiveness of the intellectual labour expended in these rationalistic projects but, in so far as the writers contribute anything solid, it derives from the *work of the law written in their hearts.* It is this natural moral consciousness that provides the awareness of right and wrong that results in doing *the things contained in the law.* This provides a meeting point between believers and unbelievers with respect to defining moral conduct but a rationalistic ethic, being restricted to general revelation, has no solution to the problem of sin. Ethics involve *willing* as well as *knowing* and it is only by reference to, and believing acceptance of, God's special revelation that we are empowered to live out God's law with a willing heart. 'For the law of the Spirit of life in Christ Jesus hath made me free from the law of sin and death. For what the law could not do, in that it was weak through the flesh, God, sending his own Son in the likeness of sinful flesh, and for sin, condemned sin in the flesh: That the righteousness of the law might be fulfilled in us, who walk not after the flesh, but after the Spirit.'[12]

## Apologetics

*Epistemology*

The fact of God's existence and certain perfections of his being *may be known*, are *manifest in* us, and have been *shown* to us by God, being *clearly seen* and *understood*. An education that studies the universe and leaves out the Creator must, therefore, necessarily suppress fundamental facts. Such an education is part of the culture that falls under the Divine censure: 'For the wrath of God is revealed from heaven against all ungodliness and unrighteousness of men, who hold the truth in unrighteousness.'[13] Such a culture is under the judgement of God and His righteous condemnation and prevents the experience of true happiness and blessedness. It is to this that the youth of our nation are consigned when education serves the interests of false religion or irreligion and man-made idols. The root of idolatry is in the imaginations of man's heart, which find expression in the intellectual inventions that are the

---

[12] Romans 8.2–4.
[13] Romans 1.18.

foundation of his culture and society. 'When they knew God, they glorified him not as God, neither were thankful; but became vain in their imaginations, and their foolish heart was darkened. Professing themselves to be wise, they became fools...'[14] The *imaginations* or reasonings of fallen man are destitute of solidity and consequently *vain* and empty. The absence of true understanding brings a shroud of darkness and when men in their degenerate state *profess* to have unlocked the secrets of the universe they become *fools* because there is no reality to their claims. This is more fundamental than the outward expressions of idolatry that emerge in consequence.

*Science*

Christianity has no quarrel with legitimate science as long as its limitations are recognised. Founders of modern science such as Sir Isaac Newton proceeded from a theistic basis in the investigation of the universe. Our awareness of ourselves and of things about us provokes thought. We investigate creation in detail by the scientific method including observation, classification, and the formulation of theories and the testing of our hypotheses. But when we consider the vastness, complexity and regular order of the universe it is inevitable that reasonable creatures such as we will be faced with *the invisible things* of God. 'The more that we know of these works, we are the more sensible that in nature there is not only an exertion of power, but an adjustment of means to an end, which is what we call wisdom, and an adjustment of means to the end of distributing happiness to all the creatures, which is the highest conception that we can form of goodness.'[15]

Most education not only fails to proceed on this theistic basis but is also antagonistic to it. (1) It stops at the stage of investigation by the scientific method and refuses to draw the necessary conclusions concerning the Creator's *eternal power and Godhead.* (2) It is however, prepared to present unproven theories as evidence against God's special revelation in the Bible as in the case of theories of origins. (3) In this way genuine scientific enterprise is distorted to give an account of the cosmos that does

---

[14] Romans 1.21–22.

[15] *Hill's Lectures, vol. i.* p.9 quoted in Robert Shaw, *op. cit.,* p. 3.

not require the Creator. (4) This attempt to provide an account of human origins without reference to God, not only goes against the knowledge of God that results in us all by observation of the universe,[16] but it goes against reason and the scientific method itself by attributing *design* to *chance*. We now know just how complex many biological systems are and the levels of interdependence required within them demonstrate amazing intricacy of design. (5) In the name of objectivity, theorising on the basis of quantitative data is applied to the social sciences, resulting in rationalistic conclusions about human behaviour that distort reality. The theoretical 'Economic Man' would be one example, which, when applied in practice results in the market-place determining, not only prices, but outcomes that require moral decisions. Christians are not alone in questioning the objectivity of such educational foundations. They arise in fact from the bias to which Paul refers which seeks an interpretation of life at variance with the *truth* to which we are all exposed concerning the Divine Architect, Benefactor, Moral Legislator and Judge.

*Positivism*

It is important to understand that the influence of Positivism in the educational curriculum is far more extensive than origins, affecting, not only the sciences, but economics, management studies, ethics and so on. Positivism is an extreme form of rationalism that denies any place to God and morality. It is assumed that there is no reality beyond the world of sense. True objectivity according to such a view involves leaving out any such considerations and accepting only what can be demonstrated by that scientific method which uses observation, classification, hypothesis framing and testing and so on. It presupposes that no positive affirmations can be made about God, because, even granting his existence, there is no revelation of him, and were there such a revelation we would not be capable of benefiting from it so as to recognise him. Such an approach is diametrically opposed to Christianity and involves a suppression of the most important part of the evidence that confronts us. Investigation of the universe leads to only one valid conclusion: the invisible God has revealed himself in his creation in such a way that the truth of his glory is

---

[16] Romans 1.20–21.

manifest in everyone, everywhere, all of the time, being understood by the things of the created universe. Only by suppression can this unmistakeable testimony be evaded. As soon as any department of the positivist curriculum claims to provide a sufficient explanation of life within the sphere of its competence it comes under the scriptural censure of foolishness: *Hath not God made foolish the wisdom of this world?*[17]

We have no quarrel with the technical facts of the physical and social sciences within their proper domain, but it would be a denial of Christ to pretend that when atheistic human theories purport to give an accurate description of the origin and meaning of life that this is some neutral zone. Any pretended competence to comprehensively fit the young or adults for a good life, while ignoring the Creator and Redeemer, is destined to be brought *to nothing*. It will not meet the needs of the individual or society. Britain has its own witness to this. Increasing technical competence has been accompanied by social decay as morality in medicine, education, business and society has become more confused. There is now, in various quarters, a degree of concern that Positivism has promoted a very narrow view of human life as a biological system, unit of labour, rational choice consumer and non-ethical agent. This is necessarily so because the very objectivity claimed by Positivism involves a bias that necessitates suppression of the moral dimension of human life so obvious in the fact of the existence of God.

*Education*

A Christian view of education is not about converting the school or college into the church. In the case of both child and adult education it is about the claims of truth and service to God. The denial of God's existence goes against the witness of our own consciences. This universal and indestructible witness, which has persisted throughout all generations, arises because of our relation to God as our Lawgiver and involves our personal accountability to him for the lives that we live. There is no inconsistency in accepting the witness of conscience to our moral accountability and, at the same time engaging in science. There is in fact a perfect consistency between the two because genuine science depends

---

[17] 1 Corinthians 2.20b.

upon the fact of Divine creation. It is because the universe manifests order and design that it can be the subject of rational investigation. There is thus no necessary obscurantism in Christian education as the achievements of Christians in education and science demonstrate. The important fact is that there is no future for a culture dependent upon a technically based education that lacks moral and spiritual reference points. This message has come through into education from Futurism and Deep Ecology. Without relevant values social decay is inescapable. But those who have discerned something of the problem cannot provide adequate answers without reference to Divine revelation in the books of creation and inspiration. Romans chapter 1 shows the inevitable degeneration arising from the denial of the true God. Paul describes some major steps in the degeneration in Romans 1.18–32. But cultural collapse in the case of the Roman Empire took place over centuries. There was a dying before the death. By comparison our lives are short. Paul did not live long enough to see the demise of Roman Paganism. For how much longer Western Society will crumble under God's judgement of worldly wisdom we cannot tell, but *it is written* that he will *destroy the wisdom of the wise*. Its different theories have their day and pass from the stage of history, sometimes in catastrophic ways. In the midst of such degeneration, education on a Christian basis can be a beacon light testifying to the consistency of the witness of the Church with genuine science, technology and sociology. Christian schools and colleges provide an opportunity to nurture an environment where legitimate scientific enterprise can proceed consistently with God's general and special revelation producing a full-orbed view of the world. Secular establishments will never foster or produce such wisdom for 'the natural man receiveth not the things of the Spirit of God: for they are foolishness unto him: neither can he know them, because they are spiritually discerned.'[18] Christian education was very seriously addressed by the reformation churches and remains a challenge for Christians today.

---

[18] 1 Corinthians 2.14.

# Chapter 13

## *The Application Of Scripture To Theological Training*

We have seen that the Holy Scriptures are the *inspired* and *infallible* Word of God written, *supremely authoritative* for doctrine, worship and practice. It necessarily follows that the essence of theological training must, therefore, be the study of the Word of God. The task of the man of God is to study the Word: 'Study to shew thyself approved unto God, a workman that needeth not to be ashamed, rightly dividing the word of truth.'[1] The task of the theological instructor is to impart the teaching of the Word: 'And the things that thou hast heard of me among many witnesses, the same commit thou to faithful men, who shall be able to teach others also.'[2] It follows that a rightly devised theological training will be focused upon the Word of God, it will derive its authority from the Word of God and it will be subject to the Word of God in its content and methods.

### The Body of Divinity: A Curriculum of Spiritual Theology

For a proper understanding of the Theology curriculum it is necessary to understand the nature of true theology, the sources for it and the branches of it. The above-mentioned title signals at the outset that true theology is more than a mere intellectual pursuit following the methodologies found in other departments of learning. The curriculum for theological training should be a curriculum of *spiritual* theology. The significance of this is explained below.

### The Nature of True Theology

In his book, *Biblical Theology*, the Puritan John Owen directs the attention of his readers to the book's title as setting out the author's

---

[1] 2 Timothy 2.15.
[2] 2 Timothy 2.2.

149

intention in the work.[3] The said title is *Biblical Theology: The History of Theology From Adam to Christ or The Nature, Origin, Development, and Study of Theological Truth, In Six Books.* Owen sees his work as setting out the nature of true theology and the method of pursuing the study of it in a God-honouring way. The title at once points to the *Biblical orientation* and *historical dimension* of true theology and the need to reckon with both of these in theological study. However Owen does not see the study of true theology as a merely intellectual exercise such as the study of philosophy. Consider the following: 'Let us proclaim it boldly – the man who is not inflamed with divine love is an outsider to all theology! Let him toil long and hard in airing of thorny questions; let him be the most avid devourer of theological books in existence; if he has this and nothing else, it is but the stronger proof that the natural beauty of God's truth has never penetrated through even the smallest chink into his mind. He is not on fire with love of divine truth, nor carried away with admiration of her beauty.'[4] The Reformed community rightly places a high estimation upon learning and for that very reason needs to take to heart Owen's point that exclusive reliance upon the intellect will never make a real theologian. True Theology is a matter of the heart and recognizes that the love of God is the starting point and terminus of the theological enterprise in accordance with the teaching of our Lord in the following passage.

> 'And one of the scribes came, and having heard them reasoning together, and perceiving that he had answered them well, asked him, Which is the first commandment of all? And Jesus answered him, The first of all the commandments is, Hear, O Israel; The Lord our God is one Lord: *And thou shalt love the Lord thy God with all thy heart, and with all thy soul, and with all thy mind, and with all thy strength: this is the first commandment.* And the second is like, namely this, Thou shalt love thy neighbour

---

[3] John Owen's Epistle to the Reader in John Owen, *Biblical Theology: The History of Theology from Adam to Christ or The Nature, Origin, Development and Study of Theological Truth, In Six Books*, Translated by Stephen P. Westcott (Morgan, PA: Soli Deo Gloria Publications, 2002) p. xxiii.

[4] *Ibid.*, p.xlvi.

as thyself. There is none other commandment greater than these. And the scribe said unto him, Well, Master, thou hast said the truth: for there is one God; and there is none other but he: And to love him with all the heart, and with all the understanding, and with all the soul, and with all the strength, and to love his neighbour as himself, is more than all whole burnt offerings and sacrifices. And when Jesus saw that he answered discreetly, he said unto him, Thou art not far from the kingdom of God. And no man after that durst ask him any question.'[5]

The study of true theology involves the Church's interaction with the Word of God in the Scriptures in order to expound the truth in a context of conflict where the Devil has sown his lies. Owen thus approves of the description 'Ecclesiastical Theology'.[6] It is no easy task to summarize Owen's thinking concerning true theology. He sums up the content of his work as follows: 'I decided after a preliminary statement concerning the name and nature of theology, to record the advances made in various ways by divine revelation, paying particular attention to the historical order of events, splitting it into its important phases since the first appearance of true theology and, also, recording the defections of many from the truth and the errors resulting therefrom, the various corruptions in the worship of the Church judged by the standard set by revelation, the many falls of the ancient church, and its restorations by grace. This would conclude with the last and final rejecting of Judaism...

'In the final section, I attempt an exposition of gospel theology itself. I have explained from the Scriptures what gospel theology is, wherein its nature lies, who alone are fitted for the study of it, how and by what method they might achieve it, what are their most likely stumbling blocks, and all this together with a consideration of the nature, establishment, and progress of true churches founded upon true theology.'[7] It will be helpful to examine what Owen has to say about the

---

[5] Mark 12. 28 – 34.

[6] John Owen, *op.cit.,* p. 6.

[7] *Ibid.,* pp. xlix.

nature of true theology, the major historical divisions that he utilizes and his view of Evangelical theology and its study.

With respect to the nature of true theology the fact that God himself is the main subject means that the methodology of human science cannot be adequate. We can have no knowledge of God except as a result of God's own self-revelation and such self-revelation is the only true and complete theology. The following can be affirmed of true theology: (1) The only *source* of true theology is the self-revelation of God. (2) The *essence* of true theology is divine truth revealed by the will of God. (3) The *content* of true theology is light and power totally self-authenticating. (4) The *end* of true theology is faith, obedience and true worship. According to Owen, Theology can thus be defined as: 'The doctrine of God with regard to Himself, His works, His will, His worship, as well as our required obedience, our future rewards and punishments, all as revealed by God Himself to the glory of His name.'[8]

The major historical divisions used by Owen in his Biblical Theology form the subject matter of his six books and are as follows: (1) Natural Theology; (2) Theology from Adam to Noah; (3) Theology from Noah to Abraham; (4) Theology from Abraham to Moses; (5) Theology from Moses to Christ and (6) Evangelical Theology. Within this historical framework he discusses the natural theology of the first man and the effects of the Fall upon it showing its insufficiency for salvation. In *Book II* he addresses the principles of the Post-Lapsarian Theology. This is followed by the origin and progress of idolatry in the period from Noah to Abraham. In *Book IV* Owen discusses the theology of Abraham and Moses and in the following book he traces the corruptions and restorations of the Mosaic Theology during the period from Moses to Christ including Ezra's reformation and the final apostasy of the Jewish Church. In *Book VI* Owen expounds the Evangelical Theology and what is necessary to its proper study.

Owen's view of Evangelical Theology must now be briefly summarized because it is highly relevant to the theological curriculum. Owen requires us to enter through the portal of humility of mind and heart quoting

---

[8] *Ibid.*, pp. 16–17.

Seneca's words: 'Many might have attained to wisdom, if they had not thought that they already had it!'[9] Christ came in the fulness of time when human wisdom and imperial power had reached their futile zenith so that by the foolishness of preaching sinners might be saved. As the eternal Word made flesh, Jesus Christ, the anointed Messiah, made known to us the will of God for our salvation. This is crucial to the whole theological enterprise: 'no one can grasp or rightly understand evangelical theology by human power or reliance on intellect, apply what outside assistance he will, for none of these things will bring him to experience the salvation to which this theology points the human mind. In this, its nature is distinct from all human sciences.'[10] The need is to be reborn spiritually and this can only be by the power of the Holy Spirit who is able to introduce us to a saving understanding of theology, enable us in spiritual worship and separate us from this world.

Owen draws a distinction between that knowledge of Biblical propositions which human reason can acquire because of the 'innate transparent clarity of the Scriptural teaching'[11] and the *true* theology. He states: 'Moreover, I concede that the principal divisions of this gospel teaching or theology, those things which concern the right worship of God, the obedience which is His due, are capable of being classified and arranged in order, sequence and method, according to the usual rules of the philosophical arts and sciences. The subject matter handed down in the gospel has a certain development and dependency, so there is nothing to prevent the interrelationships being analyzed and set out in order and, as it were, scientifically.'[12] However, in the same place he goes on to say: 'My point is that teaching, arranged and systematized in this manner, *has nothing at all in which it exceeds the purely intellectual capability of natural men. In all of this, I stress we are by no means talking of the realities themselves, but rather of methods and propositions by which it is attempted to describe those realities.'[13]

---

[9] Quoted *ibid.*, p.592.

[10] *Ibid.*, p. 603.

[11] *Ibid.*, p. 606.

[12] *Ibid.*

[13] *Ibid.*, p. 607.

Such intellectual understanding is no more than a species of Christian philosophy, superior indeed to all other philosophies because based upon absolute truth but not true *theology*. As Owen explains: 'Thus, to sum the matter up, the entirety of divine truth has been revealed in Scripture by our Lord Jesus Christ, and such is theology, if we take the term in its very widest signification. It contains propositions which are capable of systematic arrangement, and its content is open to human intellects. These revealed propositions, along with such conclusions as may legitimately be drawn from them, may be reduced to a written system and made the source material for a discipline of study. But all of this is Christian philosophy, and still lacks the hallmarks of theology in its narrower and inner signification.'[14]

Owen recognizes the value of studying Hebrew and Greek in order to gain a knowledge of the original languages of the Bible and also the disciplines that have to do with expounding language. He accepts the place of logic in right reasoning but cautions that the logic of the Holy Spirit transcends human logic with its necessary limitations. However, it is not these disciplines that make a man a true theologian, for this necessitates a personal experiential knowledge of God. 'Clearly, despite the holiness of the subject matter dealt with, we can see daily proof that the theological study in itself does not produce holiness, while the behaviour and conduct of many who have been so trained, but who are totally unworthy of the Christian name, should leave the matter beyond doubt.'[15] Owen summarizes the positive statement of his case as follows: 'To know *Him* that is true – that is *theology*...'[16] for *theology* 'is primarily spiritual wisdom.'[17] Owen later states: 'This wisdom, by which the reborn mind is illuminated with knowledge of gospel mysteries, gradually reforms the entire person in the image of heavenly truth. This is [the] most distinctive and important aspect of evangelical theology, and through it the image of God, once lost in sin, is revived afresh in man.'[18] Thus the theologian who is not being transformed by his theological studies to become more and

---

[14] *Ibid.*

[15] *Ibid.*, p.610.

[16] *Ibid.*, p.638.

[17] *Ibid.*, p.641.

[18] *Ibid.* p.643.

more Christ-like is no true theologian at all! Likewise the Church that lacks such transforming theology is no true church at all.

What advice does Owen have for the theological student? In summarizing he states: 'If you wish to be adept in this spiritual wisdom, you must daily cultivate a holy communion with God in the mystery of His gospel through the merits of Jesus Christ, and you must know by experience the power and efficiency of saving truths. These are not matters which are planted in the mind by nature or which can be gained by any amount of intellectual effort or activity! Illumination of heart, the infusion of spiritual discernment and wisdom, the revelation of the mysteries of the kingdom of Christ by the means of the Holy Spirit, the passage from outer darkness into the most wondrous light of Christ, a right to share in the wonders of wisdom and knowledge which are hidden in the Savior; what are these but empty and abhorrent words to human philosophy? Yet they are the very *origin* and *mainstay*, the pith and the marrow, of our subject!'[19] At this point both scholar and student should be arrested. We are face to face with the secret of John Owen's strength as a theologian according to his own analysis of true theology. We are caused to pause and to pray. What progress can be made without the Holy Spirit and what fruit of all our labours if they do not intensify our communion with God and our holiness of life? What hope for the church if its pastors and preachers seek to attain by intellectual endeavour what can only be accomplished by spiritual devotion? May God grant that happy balance and fruitful mingling of the two! Consider in closing Owen's definition of true theology as '*the disciplined efforts of the student's intellect (directed according to the rule of Scripture) to enhance and improve those inner spiritual gifts and saving light which constitute true, heavenly wisdom.*'[20]

**The Branches of Theology**

It will assist us in considering the branches of the tree of theology to consider what Abraham Kuyper has to say about '*The Organism of Theology in its Parts.*'[21] For Kuyper, who sees Theology as an organism

---

[19] Ibid., p. 686

[20] *Ibid.*, p.688.

[21] Abraham Kuyper, *Sacred Theology* (Wilmington, Delaware: AP & A, Undated) p. 277.

there can be no division into theological departments. An organism cannot be *divided* into parts although it is possible to *exhibit* its different parts when it is determined what they are. This is a helpful corrective against dismembering true theology. Kuyper accepts the common fourfold analysis but not as *exegetical, historical, systematic* and *practical* which are derived from activities of the human mind. He expects that our description of the parts of true theology will arise from the analysis of theology itself. He thus offers *Bibliological, Ecclesiological, Dogmatological* and *Diaconiological*. The derivation he explains as follows: 'This objective principium of division must be found in the principium of theology itself. In the development of its germ the plant of itself brings the organic spread of branches and stem. If the *Holy Scripture* is this principium of theology, it is plain that those departments should first be taken in hand which deal with *the Holy Scripture as such*; then as a second group those departments which trace the working *of the Word of God* in the life of the Church; then in a third group the departments should be combined which *reflect* the content of the Scripture *in our consciousness*; and finally a fourth group should arise from those departments which answer the question, how the working of the Word of God, subject to His ordinances, *must be maintained*.'[22] This derivation from the *object of study* corresponds to that derived from the *activities of the human mind* because in the *Bibliological* exegesis is required, in the *Ecclesiological* the historiological activity is required, in the *Dogmatological* the systematizing activity is required and in the *Diaconiological* the practical orientation requires a consideration of appropriate technique. It must be recognized, however, that these correspondences are only partial because there is more than exegesis in the study of the Bible and a measure of exegesis is required in the study of confessional statements in relation to dogma.

As to the order presented there is no need to question the priority of the *Bibliological* because Christianity is the religion of the Word. Nor need there be any dispute concerning the placing of the *Diaconiological* last for it relies upon the previous three studies; but the question may be raised as to whether the *Ecclesiological* rightly precedes the *Dogmatological*.

---

[22] *Ibid.*, p. 279.

Regarding this Kuyper comments: 'Dogma has no existence at first, but it originates only by degrees, and it is unthinkable without the Church that formulates it. If thus we would avoid the mistake of formulating our dogmatics unhistorically directly from the Scripture, but rather seek to derive it from the Scripture at the hand of the Church, then the Church as a middle-link between Bible and Dogma is absolutely indispensable.'[23] There is another justification when we recognize that there was an Old Testament Church and a New Testament Church as well as the post-apostolic Christian Church for this carries the historical research back into the times before the completion of the New Testament itself.

Kuyper's analysis described above is useful in formulating the structure of the theological curriculum, which can now be specified as follows.

## Canonical Theology

This concerns itself with *the study of the Word of God* and corresponds with Kuyper's *Bibliological*. As we have seen it is mainly but not exclusively exegetical. The description *Canonical* does not confine it to the study of the development of the Canon of Scripture but emphasizes that it is the study of the Bible *as the authoritative rule of faith and practice* and that the reason for our study is because the scripture occupies this supreme position. Professor E. J. Young includes the following under the department of Bibliology: '(1) The languages of the Bible and their cognates; (2) Biblical Exegesis; (3) Biblical History; (4) Biblical Theology; (5) Biblical Hermeneutics; (6) Biblical Antiquities, *i.e.*, the study of ancient civilizations and of archaeological research in relation to the Bible.'[24] The expected subjects would therefore be as follows:

*Scripture*

This should cover the Necessity of Scripture, the Canon and its Development, the Authority of Scripture and the Use of Scripture.

---

[23] *Ibid.*, p. 281.

[24] Edward J. Young *An Introduction to the Old Testament* (London: The Tyndale Press, 1966) footnote 2, p.15.

*Old Testament Literature*

This should cover: the Hebrew Language, the Text and Translation of the Old Testament, Introduction to the Old Testament including the authorship of the individual books, their purpose, analysis, message and theological content and finally, Exegesis.

*New Testament Literature*

This should cover: the Greek Language, the Text and Translation of the New Testament, Introduction to the New Testament including the authorship of the individual books, their purpose, analysis, message and theological content and finally Exegesis.

**Historical Theology**

This is concerned with *the Word of God working in the Church* and is as we have seen mainly Historiological. It embraces Kuyper's *Ecclesiological* with respect to the post New Testament Christian Church. It is, however, evident that there is a problem in limiting the *Ecclesiological* and Historiological to the period after the New Testament ecclesiastical history, as the first century church was just as much part of the church as the second century church. Indeed, it is common for texts on Church History to begin with the Apostolic period which was recorded in the New Testament and thus an overlap with Biblical History arises. The problem is intensified when we recognize that the Word of God working in the Church also applies to the Old Testament Church and that this would require us to resort to the Bible for the relevant data. This suggests that Biblical History and Theology have a place in Historical Theology when it spans from Adam to Christ and up to contemporary times. The following periods present themselves for consideration.

*The Conflict of Truth and Apostasy in the Early Ages of Man*

This should include the Creation, the Fall and the consequent Apostasy, the Flood and the Age of Nimrod.[25]

---

[25] See Roy Mohon, *Cosmic War Survival: The True Gospel distinguished from the Global Apostasy by reference to the Early Ages of Man* (Stockton-on-Tees: Truthzone, 2004)

*The Jewish Church in Conflict with the World*

This would include the conflict in the following ages: the Age of Egypt, the Age of Assyria, the Age of Babylon, the Age of Medo-Persia, the Age of Greece and the Age of Rome.

*The Christian Church in Conflict with the World*

The following matters should be considered under this heading: the Church of the Apostles, the Early Church in the Roman Empire, the Roman Apostasy, the Reformation, the Contemporary Church and the Future.

## Confessional Theology

This is concerned with *the Content of the Word of God systematized*. It is equivalent to Kuyper's *Dogmatological* and mainly involves systematizing. The description *Confessional* as opposed to 'Systematic' emphasizes the fact that this is the Biblical theology *ecclesiastically* systematized.

*God and Man*

Theology and Anthropology

*Redemption*

Christology and Soteriology.

*The Church*

This should include the nature of the Church, Church Government, Church Discipline, Ministry, Worship and Sacraments.

*Eschatology*

The Doctrine of the Last Things embraces both Individual Eschatology and General Eschatology.

**Ministerial Theology**

This has to do with the study of *the Application of the Word of God* and corresponds with Kuyper's *Diaconiological* being mainly concerned with technique. Its subjects are: Homiletics, Pastoral Theology, Ethics and Apologetics.

## CONCLUSION

We have completed our consideration of the Bible's necessity, qualities and use. Not only have we seen its excellencies and authority but we have considered the implications of the scriptural doctrine for the way in which we ought to conduct ourselves in Church, daily life and learning. As long as our nation continues on in unbelief, it will be denied the rich blessings that arise in consequence of living by the Word of God. May the brief survey given in this book stir the reader to a realization of the significance of the Bible for a purposeful and God glorifying life. May it give to you that appreciation of the Holy Scriptures expressed by the Psalmist in the following words:

'O how love I thy law! It is my meditation all the day.'[26]

---

[26] Psalm 119.97.

# Glossary

### Apographs and Autographs

In the theological literature, the manuscripts given in the first place by inspiration are called *autographs*. The word *apographs* is used to describe the manuscripts copied *from* (*apo*) the Hebrew and Greek manuscripts that had been given by inspiration of the Holy Spirit through chosen men such as prophets and apostles. These latter manuscripts are called *autographs* to distinguish them from the *apographs*.

### Dynamic equivalence

'The principle of translation that attempts to recreate on the reader of the receptor language the impact the original text had on the original recipients, without being bound literally to reproduce the words as nearly as possible. (The translator then assumes the role of interpreter, to determine the thought intended in the original. This often results in an interpretative paraphrase that has little or no relationship to the original language text.)'[1]

### Extant Manuscripts

The word 'extant' is used to describe those copies of Scripture that have survived to the present day and are therefore available for scholars to consult. Such manuscripts vary in completeness and reliability. The vast majority support the so-called Byzantine tradition that underlies the *Received Text*.

### Formal equivalence

'The principle of translation that accepts *every* word of Holy Scripture as being of divine origin and therefore takes into account *every* word in the original language to ensure that as far as possible the grammar, the

---

[1] Word List, *Quarterly Record*, April to June 2005, pp. 12–15.

form, the vocabulary and the syntax of the Hebrew and Greek are followed in the translation ('As literal as possible, as free as necessary').[2]

## General Revelation

'The general revelation of God is prior to His special revelation in point of time. It does not come to man in the form of verbal communications, but in the facts, the forces, and the laws of nature, in the constitution and operation of the human mind, and in the facts of experience and history.'[3]

## Inspiration

The essential idea of inspiration in the original Greek is not 'breathed *into*', as the English word might suggest, but 'breathed *out*.' The Greek word literally means 'God-breathed.' Thus Scripture is the *Word of God* written.

## Plenary Inspiration

This term is used to state that the inspiration of the Bible is full and complete, every part of it is inspired. It is closely associated with verbal inspiration, which means that inspiration extends to the very words used to convey the ideas.

## Received Text

'The various editions of the Received Text, or *Textus Receptus*, of the sixteenth and seventeenth centuries represented (with a few very minor differences) the Byzantine Text-type. Erasmus edited five editions of the New Testament text from 1516 to 1535, and others were produced by Estienne (the Latin form of his name is Stephanus), Beza, and Bonaventure and Abraham Elzevir. The phrase 'Received Text' comes from the Preface to Elzevirs' second edition (1633). This title has been used over the centuries to classify all the printed editions of the Greek text of the same provenance.'[4]

---

[2] *Ibid.*

[3] Louis Berkhof, *Summary of Christian Doctrine* (Edinburgh: The Banner of Truth Trust, 1960) p. 11.

[4] Word List, *Quarterly Record*, April to June 2005, pp. 12–15.

## Special Revelation

'The Bible is pre-eminently the book of God's special revelation, a revelation in which the facts and words go hand in hand, the words interpreting the facts and the facts giving substance to the words.'[5]

---

[5] Louis Berkhof, *op. cit.*, p. 12.

# Bibliography

## Bible Versions

Quotations are from the *Authorised (King James) Version of the Bible* (London: Trinitarian Bible Society) except where otherwise indicated. Reference has also been made to the *Holy Bible: Revised Version* (London: The British and Foreign Bible Society, 1959), *The Holy Bible: New International Version, Containing The Old Testament and The New Testament* (London: Hodder and Stoughton, 1979) and *The Holy Bible: Revised Authorised Version* (London: Samuel Bagster, 1982).

## Other Literature

ALEXANDER, J. A. (1984) *A Commentary on the Acts of the Apostles* (Edinburgh: The Banner of Truth Trust)

BERKHOF, L. (1963) *Systematic Theology* (Edinburgh: The Banner of Truth Trust)

BRIDGES, Charles (1968) *A Commentary on Proverbs* (Edinburgh: The Banner of Truth Trust)

BROWN, John (1964) *An Exposition of the Epistle to the Hebrews* (Edinburgh: The Banner of Truth Trust)

BRUGGEN, Jakob van (1979) *The Ancient Text of the New Testament* (Winnipeg, Manitoba: Premier)

BUNYAN, John (1904) *The Pilgrim's Progress* (London: Henry Frowde)

CALVIN, J (1962) *Institutes of the Christian Religion*, Volume One (London: James Clarke & Co., Limited)

CALVIN, John (2003) *Commentary on the Book of the Prophet Isaiah, Volume IV* (Grand Rapids: Baker Book House)

CONFESSION OF FAITH OF THE WESTMINSTER ASSEMBLY OF DIVINES, THE in S. W. Carruthers (ed.), *The Westminster Confession of Faith* (Manchester: R. Aikman & Son, 1937)

DICKSON, David (1981) *A Brief Exposition of the Evangel of Jesus Christ According to Matthew* (Edinburgh: The Banner of Truth Trust)

GELDENHUYS, Norval (1975) *Commentary on the Gospel of Luke: The English Text with Introduction Exposition and Notes* (Grand Rapids: Wm. B. Eerdmans Publishing Company)

HENDRIKSEN, William (1964) *A Commentary on I & II Timothy and Titus* (Edinburgh: The Banner of Truth Trust)

HENDRIKSEN, William (1969) *The Gospel of John* (Edinburgh: The Banner of Truth Trust)

HENRY, Matthew (Undated) *An Exposition of the Old and New Testament, Vol. VI. – Acts to Revelation* (London: James Nisbet & Co., Limited)

HILLS, Edward F. (1993) *The King James Version Defended* (Des Moines, Iowa: The Christian Research Press)

HODGE, A. A. (1964) *The Confession of Faith: A Handbook of Christian Doctrine Expounding The Westminster Confession* (Edinburgh: The Banner of Truth Trust)

HODGE, Charles (1960) *Systematic Theology* (London: James Clarke & Co. Ltd.)

HODGE, Charles (1964) *A Commentary on the First Epistle to the Corinthians* (Edinburgh: The Banner of Truth Trust)

KUYPER, Abraham (Undated) *Sacred Theology* (Wilmington, Delaware: AP & A)

MARTIN, Robert P. (1997) *Accuracy of Translation: The Primary Criterion in Evaluating Bible Versions with special reference to the New International Version* (Edinburgh: The Banner of Truth Trust)

MERRILL, Eugene H. (1975) *An Historical Survey of the Old Testament* (Nutley, New Jersey: The Craig Press)

METZGER, Bruce M. (1975) *A Textual Commentary on The Greek New Testament* (London: United Bible Societies)

MOHON, Roy (2004) *Cosmic War Survival: The True Gospel distinguished from the Global Apostasy by reference to the Early Ages of Man* (Stockton-on-Tees: Truthzone)

MURRAY, John (1968) *The Epistle to the Romans* (Grand Rapids, Michigan: Wm. B. Eerdmans Publishing Co.)

OWEN John (2002) *Biblical Theology: The History of Theology from Adam to Christ or The Nature, Origin, Development and Study of Theological Truth, In Six Books*, Translated by Stephen P. Westcott (Morgan, PA: Soli Deo Gloria Publications)

PINK, Arthur W. Pink (1954) *An Exposition of Hebrews* (Grand Rapids: Baker Book House)

RIDDERBOS, Herman N. (1968) *The Epistle of Paul to the Churches of Galatia: The English Text with Introduction, Exposition and Notes* (Grand Rapids: Wm. B. Eerdmans Publishing Co.)

SCRIVENER, F. H. A. (1881) *The New Testament in the Original Greek According to the Text followed in the Authorised Version together with the Variations Adopted in the Revised Version* (Cambridge: University Press)

SHAW, Robert (1973) *The Reformed Faith: An Exposition of the Confession of Faith of the Westminster Assembly of Divines* (Inverness: Christian Focus Publications)

STRONG, James (1990) *The New Strong's Exhaustive Concordance of the Bible* (London: Thomas Nelson Publishers)

THOMAS, I. D. E. (1997) *The Golden Treasury of Puritan Quotations* (Edinburgh: The Banner of Truth Trust)

TURRETIN, Francis (1992) *Institutes of Elenctic Theology,* Volume 1 (Phillipsburg, New Jersey: P&R Publishing)

WARFIELD, Benjamin Breckinridge (1991) *The Westminster Assembly and its Work* (Grand Rapids, Michigan: Baker Book House)

WESTMINSTER CONFESSION OF FAITH, THE, (1937) ed. S. W. Carruthers (Manchester: R. Aikman & Son)

WILLIAMS, P. J. Williams (2004) *Early Syriac Translation Technique and the Textual Criticism of the Greek Gospels* (Gorgias Press)

YOUNG, Edward J. (1963) *Thy Word is Truth: Some Thoughts on the Biblical Doctrine of Inspiration* (Edinburgh: The Banner of Truth Trust)

YOUNG, Edward J. (1966) *An Introduction to the Old Testament* (London: The Tyndale Press)

# Index

**Other books published by Twoedged Sword Publications**

*Try the spirits: volume 1*

Cecil Andrews

ISBN 0-9547205-2-0

- Was C S Lewis truly 'Our greatest Christian writer'?

- Philip Yancey—'turning the grace of God into lasciviousness'?

- Alpha—Attend or Avoid?

When the writer first formed 'Take Heed' Ministries some fourteen years ago most of the warnings issued on spiritual deception would have referred to matters outside of professing Christendom. Today the spiritual make-up of that professing Christendom is both very different and very dangerous. There has been a biblically-predicted (1 Timothy 4:1 and 2 Timothy 4:3) marked decline in discernment amongst professing Christians and the result is that the questionable views of certain apologists, authors and advocates, who are viewed by many as Christian, have increased dramatically both in popularity and influence. This book is an attempt to bring biblical truth to bear on three such current dangers that are deceiving many.

*Try the spirits: volume 2*

Cecil Andrews

ISBN 0-9547205-5-5

- Catholic Catechism—some non-Christian teachings
- 'Father' McCafferty—Catholic but not Christian
- Alister McGrath—misrepresenting the Catholic Catechism?
- ECT Ireland—the myth of Evangelicals and Catholics Together in Ireland
- Evangelising Roman Catholics

Almost five hundred years ago the Roman Catholic domination of professing Christendom was broken as God, by His Spirit, moved in the hearts, minds and understanding of many who had found no peace with God through their adherence to, and reliance upon, priestly Roman Catholic ritual. The rediscovery of the great biblical truth of 'justification through faith alone in Christ alone' became central to what is known as The Reformation. Today, many appear to have forgotten the spiritual lessons of that crucial period and for a number of decades now Romanism has once more been rising to a position of dominance like the proverbial Phoenix from the ashes. This bodes ill for the eternal well-being of countless souls. May the One who alone has saved His people from their sins be pleased to use this little volume to counter the claims of a false anti-Christian system that is so loved by the world today.

***Condemned, Condoned or Confused?***

*The Contemporary World in the Light of God's Word*

Timothy Cross, BA (Hons), BD (Hons), Th.D.

ISBN 0-9547205-3-9

- Bad language
- The cult of the celebrity
- The family
- The status and role of women
- Homosexuality
- Gambling
- Alcohol

This book considers these, and many other prominent aspects of our modern world, in the light of God's Word—which is the correct standard by which to *prove all things* (1 Thessalonians 5:21). Sadly, when our contemporary society is tested in the light of God's unchanging Word it is often *weighed in the balances, and... found wanting* (Daniel 5:27). But the situation is not hopeless, for the Bible shows us where we have strayed from God's way and how we can return to God's way, the only way to true happiness, peace and eternal life. Only the Bible can make us truly wise, as only the Bible can impart the wisdom of God.

## Some Postcards from John

*2 and 3 John for today*

Timothy Cross, BA (Hons), BD (Hons), Th.D.

ISBN 0-9547205-7-1

The 'postcards' that John wrote to the churches of 2 and 3 John are packed full of useful instruction and exhortation. John sent these 'postcards' on ahead of hoped for, and longed for face to face visits: in 2 John to *the elect lady and her children* and in 3 John to *the beloved Gaius.*

Both churches had their problems. The problem in the church of 2 John concerned deceiving deviants from outside the church — *men who will not acknowledge the coming of Jesus Christ in the flesh*, whilst the problem addressed in 3 John was concerned mainly with a dreadful dictator from within the church — *Diotrephes, who likes to put himself first, does not acknowledge my authority.* These problem personalities from the first century will ring many present-day bells with us in the twenty-first century.

In John's 'postcards', we encounter doctrine, duty, affirmation of truth, and warning against error. We meet love and discipline along with affection and sternness. Overriding everything, as everywhere in the Bible, we glimpse something of the supernatural glory of God in contrast with the sinful humanity He sent His Own Son to save.

At the end of each chapter there is a set of thought-provoking and stimulating questions, each of which could be the subject of a Bible study group.

*An Exposition of I Peter Chapter I*

Robert A. Penney B.D., D.Min.

ISBN 0-9547205-4-7

The lessons that Peter brings to us might have been written with our current times in mind, such is the relevance and agelessness of Scripture. In expounding these great truths, the author considers the following subjects:

- Apostleship

- Election

- Worship, Mercy and Lively Hope

- The Preservation of the believer

- Heaviness

- The Trial of Faith

- Unseen but Loved

- The Desire of Prophets

- The Desire of Angels

- Holiness

- Redeemed by Blood

- The Christian's Hope and Faith in God's Power

- The Transient Nature of our Existence and the Eternal Nature of the Word of God

- Vain Glory: The Enduring Word

*An Exposition of II Peter chapter 3*

Robert A. Penney B.D., D.Min.

ISBN 0-9547205-9-8

The old adage says: "Your bible is more up-to-date than your morning's newspaper." Such a statement was never more true than when applied to this third chapter of Peter's second epistle. It has to do with the present state of affairs and gives us a brief insight into the end time and also a glimpse of the nature of the future kingdom. To live amid this present godless world with such Scriptures saturating our minds and our souls is richness indeed and fills the believer with hope, confidence and faith in these modern times of unbelief and apostasy.

These addresses are sent forth trusting that the result will be the strengthening of all who read them, that hope may be instilled within those who may be discouraged in these wicked times and that even thrill and excitement may be aroused as one contemplates the believer's lot in this present evil world and the glories which will follow. Nothing is more needful today than for the Christian to be encouraged in the things he has most surely believed.

The author has written this small book to encourage Christians to rejoice in the hope of their high calling and to consider the eventual triumph of Christ and His Church over Satan and his forces and over the ungodliness of men which is so characteristic of these last days. But the chapter under consideration is also full of warnings for the believer—the appearance of evil on an unprecedented scale, the ultimate wrath of God in judgment upon it all and how we must get back to spiritual basics by heeding the teaching of the apostles and prophets.

*A Faith for the Times*

Robert A. Penney B.D., D.Min.

ISBN 0-9547205-8-X

Only One Message • Liberty in the Spirit • The Power of the Spirit • The Demonstration of the Spirit • The Power of God • Impossibilities • Divine Revelation • Divine Commission • Departed Glory • The Flickering Lamp • Leadership • The Function of the Local Church • Treasures of Darkness • Fire! • Scotland's Finest Hour • Righteousness

Dr Robert A. Penney addresses the problems of a people that has turned its back on God: materialism, moral depravity, humanism, philosophy, sin in high places. He reflects on the ways in which God dealt with the people of Israel and its leaders, the early New Testament Church as well as some of the problems in the modern Church.

'When you read the Bible and get to know it thoroughly, you will find that it is a book that speaks to every age and generation, because mankind remains the same in all its essential qualities, and God remains the same.'—Dr. Martyn Lloyd-Jones

Dr Penney spent over twenty years as a Probation Officer in the Birmingham courts. On early retirement he studied at the Scottish Congregational College and New College, Edinburgh, whilst serving as an assistant to the late Dr Nelson Gray at Portobello Congregational Church. He pastored Beith Congregational Church, Ayrshire, for a short period before resigning to devote himself to writing and itinerant ministry. He now lives in Kirkintilloch, his home town, near Glasgow.

*The Christology of Philippians 2:6–11*

*An examination of the Person and Work of Christ*

M. W. J. Phelan, B.Th., M.Th., Th.D.

ISBN 0-9547205-1-2

By accepting that all the Scriptures centre on Christ; that all the believer's hopes centre upon Him; and that we are acceptable to God only through Him and His Work, all true believers practice Christology. This book exposes the so-called Kenotic Theology as a falsehood. This doctrine teaches that the Deity of Christ was compromised when He took our flesh. The danger of this doctrine is made worse by the fact that it may seem to be correct, but, as this book reveals, it is based upon a fundamental misunderstanding. Many believers will find this book to be of real interest and benefit, especially as it could easily be used as the basis for a small study group, in which believers may explore together the exhilarating truths dealt with by the writer.

*The Inspiration of the Pentateuch*
*or*
*The Graf-Wellhausen Fallacy*

*An examination of the origins of the Torah, the inadequacies and contradictions of cynical Source Criticism, and the merits of Faithful Source, and Form Criticism.*

M. W. J. Phelan, B.Th., M.Th., Th.D., Ph.D.

ISBN 0-9547205-6-3

Christianity claims the Bible is a comprehensive collection of truths concerning the nature and purposes of God, and the nature and destiny of mankind. It claims that this Divinely Inspired, and therefore, utterly inerrant revelation was transmitted to us through the New Testament. However, this collection of documents rests upon the Hebrew Canon, or Old Testament, and the very foundation of the Hebrew Canon, is the Torah, or Pentateuch, or Five-Books-Of-Moses; namely, Genesis, Exodus, Leviticus, Numbers, and Deuteronomy. It is the Pentateuch that has been the target of the most unremitting assaults of sceptics and critics down the years, and the Book of Genesis has suffered the most brutal of these attacks. It is these assaults upon the Pentateuch that form the subject of this book.

*The Genesis 'Gap Theory'*

*Its Credibility and Consequences*

M. W. J. Phelan, B.Th., M.Th., Th.D., Ph.D.

ISBN 1-905447-02-7

The interpretation of Genesis 1:1–2 has taxed the minds of exegetes for many years. The controversy has centred upon whether or not there is a chronological gap of unspecified duration within the compass of what, at first glance, seems to be continuous narrative. This proposed gap is the basis of what might be termed theories-of-accommodation. By some the proposed gap is used to accommodate the alleged vast ages of cosmic, geological, and biological evolution, and has certain similarities with the theory that views the days of Genesis 1, not as literal days representing but one complete rotation of the earth upon its axis, but as entire epochs, during which the earth was subject to profound, but extremely slow evolutionary change. This is a view frequently advocated by so-called Theistic-Evolutionists, who seek to harmonise Scripture with human wisdom in the form of evolutionary dogma.

The facts are that;

1) the six days of Genesis 1 are each defined as comprising but one 'evening and morning' (verses 5, 8, 13, 19, 23, and 31),

2) Exodus 20:11 and 31:17 state that the basis of the seven-day week which regulates our calendar still, is the hexameron, or six days of creation followed by the Sabbath rest,

3) death did not exist before Adam, and came through Adam (Romans 5:12), ruling out the possibility of millions of years of plant and animal deaths before man, and,

4) the concept of the history of the events of Genesis 1, being greater in duration than all the rest of Scripture history taken together, and of it outlasting it by a truly prodigious amount which the adoption of an evolutionary time-scale would demand, is absolutely contrary to the conceptual basis of the Word-of-God.

The desire to accommodate entire epochs such as are suggested by evolutionists within a chronological gap to be located within Genesis 1:1–2 then should not be a serious consideration for sincere students of the Word.

But the proposed gap is used also to accommodate the Luciferic Rebellion and Fall. It is taught by believers in this view that the original creation was marred, if not ruined altogether by this rebellion, or by a Divine Judgement which fell upon the earth as a consequence of it, and that the hexameron details the actions of God in restoring the, by then, ruined earth.

Finally, there are those who see such a gap accommodating *both* evolutionary epochs, and the Luciferic Rebellion.

What the sincere student of God's Word needs to know is; whether or not there is any real basis in the Scriptures themselves for the existence of such a gap, or whether the proposal is based only upon human speculation. It is the authors' aim to address this question.

*The Integrity of Isaiah: New evidence of single authorship*

*A practical demonstration of the literary unity of the book of Isaiah*

M. W. J. Phelan, B.Th., M.Th., Th.D., Ph.D.

ISBN 1-905447-03-5

For over two thousand years the book of Isaiah was accepted as the exclusive work of the son of Amoz, the friend of Hezekiah. The translators of the Septuagint regarded the book as a single work. The well-known discovery at Qumran in 1947 of two different copies of Isaiah also testifies to its unity. One of these scrolls is virtually complete and is normally dated to the late second century B.C.E.

The New Testament adds its very considerable, and for the believer, decisive weight to the traditional viewpoint, as may be seen from the eighty-seven occasions where it cites the prophet's words. In no less than twenty-one of these instances, the quotation from the book is accompanied by a reference to the prophet Isaiah by name.

In addition to this, the Masoretic Text, the standard Hebrew text of the Hebrew Canon, and the unanimous testimony of all the ancient texts, versions, Jewish traditions, and the early Christian Church, report the book to be a single work.

At the end of the eighteenth century however, this view that had held sway for millennia began to be challenged. Isaiah, it was asserted was a compilation by different authors, and various so-called proofs of this were brought forth by the critics. Since then, this view-point has gained a massive momentum so that it is now considered to be the orthodox scholarly position. We are assured that critical scholarship has demonstrated the separate existence of the work of no less than three authors, usually referred to as Proto-Isaiah, Deutero-Isaiah, and Trito-Isaiah.

The issues raised by this challenge to the traditional belief, are firstly and obviously, that the Hebrew Canon is charged with containing pseudonymous works, but secondly, and more importantly, the authority of the New Testament is gravely undermined, as the twenty-one occasions where Isaiah is referred to by name, relate to every section of the book, and, therefore, to all three of the modernist's authors.

Either the evangelists and Paul were unaware of what has supposedly been unearthed by the critics, and thereby face the charge of gross ignorance; or they were not ignorant at all, but accommodated themselves to the prejudices of those they wrote for, and, thereby, knowingly and deliberately maintained a falsehood. For believers then, the matter is not merely of academic interest, but affects his or her faith in the Inspiration of the New Testament. A New Testament that through ignorance or deliberate policy propagates and maintains a falsehood cannot be Divinely Inspired, or relied upon as our guide in the most vital issues which confront us all, the issues of life and death in their eternal dimensions. Clearly then the matter must be resolved, and either the New Testament, or the views of the critics must be abandoned; the matter is as stark as that.

***Things which must shortly come to pass***

*A study of Revelation*

Paul Rose

ISBN 0-9547205-0-4

The things John wrote in the book of Revelation were revealed to him by the Lord Jesus Christ Himself. They are *things which must shortly come to pass* (Revelation 1:1). Many Revelation prophesies have already been fulfilled and those who keep an eye on the political arena can see the way being prepared for the fulfilment of more Revelation prophecies. In the writer's opinion we should study Revelation with renewed enthusiasm because *these things must shortly come to pass.*


***Angels Everwatching***

*One family's testimony of God's protection and mercy*

Robert Baghurst, Rosemarie Baghurst, Timothy Baghurst, Amy Baghurst

ISBN 1-905447-00-0

"Liberia's motto has always intrigued me... 'For the Love of Liberty brought us here.' It has always been their boast to be the first African nation that was free, all the others having first been colonised. Actually this has been to their disadvantage since they had no strong Western influence to educate, support, and give them a good basis from which to work and grow. To the contrary, they have always been a poor nation, proud to be free, but wholly enslaved to the animistic traditions which they tenaciously hold."

The Liberian civil war erupted in December 1989, when the National Patriotic Front of Liberia (NPFL), a military force led by Charles Ghankay Taylor, a former official of the Liberian government, invaded Liberia from the Ivory Coast. He received the assistance of mercenaries from other nations, with many recruits from the Mano and Gio ethnic groups. The Baghurst family found themselves in the path of this force and for a time found themselves captives. During their experience they learned that the "angel of the LORD encampeth round about them that fear him, and delivereth them" (Psalm 34:7). This is that story.

## The Army and I

*An account of life in the Army as a non-combatant Christian during the Second World War*

Robert B. Carter

ISBN 1-905447-01-9

This is an account of one individual's impressions and experiences in the Second World War. It is based on the author's memory and on a notebook in which, throughout the war, he entered names and addresses, locations, train journeys, leave dates, rates of pay, and so on. Many have recorded their experiences during those terrible years, but few have written of service with non-combatant status within the Army.

He whose words can never pass away said:

> "Render to Caesar the things that are Caesar's and to
> God the things that are God's" (Mark 12:17).

In times of national danger, Caesar inevitably tends to enlarge his claims upon us and it is good if there are statutory safeguards. Throughout the history of the church, there has been difficulty for many in discovering where, in practice, the boundary between these two responsibilities lies. The conscience of the believer is enlightened by, and subject to, the Word of God, but as one Christian said when called to answer before the Great Council in Zurich in the early part of the 16th century:

> "Do not oppress my conscience, for faith is a free gift
> of
> God's mercy and is not to be interfered with by
> anyone."

May any who read this record be encouraged to commit their lives to Him who "worketh all things after the counsel of His own will" (Ephesians 1:11).

*Einstein's Predicament*

*A New Approach to the Speed of Light*

Francis Pym and Clifford Denton

ISBN 1-905447-06-X

The authors reopen an important question.

'How does light work?'

100 years ago, Einstein published his famous article on light. Despite being found incompatible with other theories, it has largely been accepted by the scientific community and given impetus to much that is useful in our understanding of the universe.

Was Einstein right however, in saying that a medium in space to carry light could be ignored without consequences? Most people are not able either to understand or challenge his assumptions, yet, with some simple maths the authors make a strong case to return to absolutes in space and time and demonstrate that Einstein may have made some serious errors. They therefore propose bypassing relativity theory without losing its valid results and offer a logical alternative that restores meaning to time, length, speed of light, and size and age of the universe.

Francis Pym, as a member of the Royal Institute of British Architects, won an important Architectural Competition and other awards, having qualified at the Architectural Association, London.

Clifford Denton studied mathematics at the University of Cambridge and obtained his Doctorate at the University of Oxford. His research included the identification of and educational provision for gifted children in mathematics.

*Bible Bites*

*Food for thought every day*

Keith Foster

ISBN 1-905447-08-6

Quite often we associate the term 'devotional' with warm fuzzy thoughts; pleasant little nothings which give us a short-lived buzz that we soon forget as we go through our normal routines. However, true devotion is radically different from this idea. The word 'devote' literally means to give entirely and completely. It is rooted in the concept of a vow. In the Bible, to devote something to God means to give it entirely to Him. The aim of these devotionals, or 'devos', is to challenge you to do just that. Are you devoting your studies, your friendships, and your family time… whatever, to God every day?

These thoughts and challenges flow from the pages of Scripture through the life of the author, Keith Foster. He practices what he preaches. It is not the author's intent to make us complacent with pleasant platitudes, but to challenge all of us to become fully devoted to the Lord Jesus Christ.

Keith Foster is responsible for youth and family ministries at Paulsgrove Baptist Church, Portsmouth. His work involves school and college Christian unions, Religious education classes, community outreach and church wide youth events.

Keith has been married to Lesley for 22 years and they have two teenage daughters, Becky and Rachel aged 18 and 14.

*Apocalypse Facts and Fantasies*

*Truths Tested and Errors Exposed by God's Gracious Guarantees to Israel*

Donald C B Cameron B.Th., MA, Ph.D., Cert.Ed.

ISBN 1-905447-07-8

The author believes there is a unique, God-given key to help us unravel the conflicting prophetic programmes which abound. We might define this key as Israel's guaranteed future as a nation and race, based upon God's faithful promises. This does not disallow Jews from becoming Church members in the present age. God's promises to Israel include both conditional and unconditional, both short term and long term, both fulfilled and unfulfilled, both blessings and cursings. Any scheme which does not allow God to fulfil His unconditional promises is fatally flawed. Where God has promised ultimate forgiveness and restoration, let no man dare to know better!

This book examines what the Bible says about Israel and the future, then applies this to different teachings, demonstrating that those schools of prophecy which selectively deny God's promises to Israel effectively invalidate themselves. If we fail to recognise the significance of the vast number of prophetic passages in Scripture which refer to Israel, we will fail to perceive the overall programme of latter day events.

Such terms as "The Four Horses of the Apocalypse", "The Mark of the Beast" and "The Battle of Armageddon" tend to be better known to film directors than to churchmen. There is a need to rectify this imbalance and to address two dangerous extremes. One is the teaching that such things are the province of pessimists, and that predicted calamities were deliberate exaggerations on the part of prophets to drive lessons home. The other is the scoffing attitude foretold by Peter, leading to apathy akin to that of Jesus' First Coming. None should willingly share the condemnation of the two disciples returning to Emmaus on the evening of the Resurrection day: "O foolish ones, and slow of heart to believe in all that the prophets have spoken" (Luke 24:25). Their folly had led to unnecessary heartbreak.

A further need is for enquiring Jews to receive assurances that there are Christians who do not believe that they as a nation have been for ever dismissed from God's future plans, as some teach, and that their displacement from the centre of God's purposes over the centuries by the largely Gentile Church has a strict time limit. They need to be re-assured that God has beautifully co-ordinated plans for all His people. In the meantime they may be individually welcomed into the Church on the same basis as everyone else. There never has been, never will be and never can be any means of salvation for sinners than through the blood of the Lamb, Christ Jesus, shed on Calvary's Cross. Jesus is described as the Lamb more often in Revelation than in any other book of the Bible. God has never saved by any other means. Whether one is Jew or Gentile, repentance and faith are required in order that this redeeming blood may be applied.

As an Educational Officer, Donald Cameron commanded the Army's Russian Language Wing and was British Liaison Officer to the Soviet Military Liaison Mission in West Germany. He has been a leadership training consultant, and has himself been in leadership in several churches.

Printed in the United Kingdom
by Lightning Source UK Ltd.
110068UKS00001B/409-441